STUDY PROJECT ON
SOCIAL RESEARCH
AND DEVELOPMENT
VOLUME 5

Knowledge and Policy:
The Uncertain Connection

Laurence E. Lynn, Jr., *Editor*

Study Project on Social Research and Development
Assembly of Behavioral and Social Sciences
National Research Council

NATIONAL ACADEMY OF SCIENCES
Washington, D.C.   1978

NOTICE: The project that is the subject of this report was approved by the Governing Board of the National Research Council, whose members are drawn from the Councils of the National Academy of Sciences, the National Academy of Engineering, and the Institute of Medicine. The members of the Committee responsible for the report were chosen for their special competences and with regard for appropriate balance.

This report has been reviewed by a group other than the authors according to procedures approved by a Report Review Committee consisting of members of the National Academy of Sciences, the National Academy of Engineering, and the Institute of Medicine.

Library of Congress Cataloging in Publication Data

National Research Council. Study Project on Social Research and Development.
  Knowledge and policy.

  Includes bibliographies.
  1. Social science research—United States—Addresses, essays, lectures. 2. Federal aid to research—United States—Addresses, essays, lectures. 3. Policy sciences—Addresses, essays, lectures. 4. United States—Social policy—Addresses, essays, lectures. I. Lynn, Laurence E., 1937-   II. Title.
H62.N3625   1978   300'.1'8   78-1960

ISBN 0-309-02732-2

Available from:
Printing and Publishing Office
National Academy of Sciences
2101 Constitution Avenue, N.W.
Washington, D.C. 20418

Printed in the United States of America

STUDY PROJECT ON SOCIAL RESEARCH AND DEVELOPMENT

DONALD E. STOKES (*Chairman*), Woodrow Wilson School of Public and International Affairs, Princeton University

ROBERT MCC. ADAMS, Oriental Institute, University of Chicago (member until July 1975)

FREDERICK O'R. HAYES, Lexington, Massachusetts

LESTER B. LAVE, Graduate School of Industrial Administration, Carnegie-Mellon University

LAURENCE E. LYNN, JR., John F. Kennedy School of Government, Harvard University

GUY ORCUTT, Department of Economics, Yale University

MICHAEL D. REAGAN, University of California, Riverside

GEORGE TANHAM, Rand Corporation

ROBIN M. WILLIAMS, JR., Department of Sociology, Cornell University

iii

58877 195

95

Foreword

This volume was prepared by the National Research Council for the National Science Foundation (NSF). At the request of NSF's Science and Technology Policy Office in 1974, the National Research Council agreed to undertake a study of the organization and management of social research and development throughout the federal government. To carry out this task, the Study Project on Social Research and Development was established within the Assembly of Behavioral and Social Sciences of the National Research Council.

The work of the Study Project includes six volumes, to be published in 1978–1979:

Volume 1: *The Federal Investment in Knowledge of Social Problems* (Study Project Report)
Volume 2: *The Funding of Social Knowledge Production and Application: A Survey of Federal Agencies*
Volume 3: *Studies in the Management of Social R&D: Selected Policy Areas*
Volume 4: *Studies in the Management of Social R&D: Selected Issues*
Volume 5: *Knowledge and Policy: The Uncertain Connection*
Volume 6: *The Uses of Basic Research: Case Studies in Social Science*

Acknowledgments

In commissioning these papers and preparing them for publication, I have benefited from the generous support and advice of the members of the Committee on the Study Project on Social Research and Development. I would also like to acknowledge the outstanding editorial talents of Eugenia Grohman, who edited several of the papers, and particularly of Chris McShane, who edited several of the papers and prepared the entire volume for production.

Laurence E. Lynn, Jr.

Contents

Introduction

LAURENCE E. LYNN, JR.

In 1976, the federal government invested more than $1.8 billion in social research and development (R&D)—i.e., in research, statistics, evaluations, demonstrations, and experiments—relating to the identification and solution of social problems. Although the need for large-scale federal support of social R&D is widely accepted, questions concerning its relevance to the making of social policy have become more insistent in recent years. What are we learning? Who is making effective use of what we learn?

The beginning of systematic federal support for social R&D can perhaps be traced to the creation of the Federal Bureau of Ethnology in 1881. During the following four decades, motivated by the Progressive Era's concern for social problems and the need for scientific advice generated by World War I, federal support for social R&D emerged in recognizable form. The Depression Era's social problems and World War II further stimulated federal spending for social research, which reached $53 million in 1937 and was more than $60 million by 1953 (Archibald 1967). Growth was slow during the 1950s, then accelerated sharply during the 1970s, stimulated by another burst of governmental energy to solve social problems; the present level of spending was reached in the early 1970s.

THE IMPORTANCE OF "RELEVANCE"

As federal support for social R&D reached significant levels, controversies began. To oversimplify a complex history, there have been

1

two principal sources of controversy: legislators distrustful of "social engineers" who promote radical ideas or pursue irrelevant academic interests, and social scientists worried that dependence on government might compromise their objectivity.

An early manifestation of this controversy was contained in the 1938 report of the National Resource Committee, *Research—A National Resource*. This report recommended that "research within the Government and by non-governmental agencies which cooperate with the Government be so organized and conducted as to avoid the possibilities of bias through subordination in any way to policy-making and policy-enforcing." A series of quasi-official reports, beginning with the 1938 report of the National Resource Committee, have discussed national policies for the support of research to solve complex social problems. These reports have urged the federal government to play a major role in supporting social R&D and have discussed a variety of the problems that arise when the government undertakes such support. (See, for example, President's Science Advisory Committee 1962; U.S. Congress, House 1967; National Research Council 1968, 1969; National Science Foundation 1969.)

In the early 1970s, federal policy-making officials whose agencies supported social R&D became a relatively new source of controversy. Many of these officials believed that the *raison d'etre* for the growing amounts of money being spent was the production of knowledge that would be useful in their policy-making roles. Based on their experience in looking for and using knowledge from research, however, they expressed doubts that federally supported social R&D produced much useful knowledge or that usable knowledge was actually used often enough to justify the expense of obtaining it.

For example, former secretary of Health, Education, and Welfare (HEW) Elliot Richardson, whose department accounted for nearly half of federally supported social R&D, observed (U.S. HEW 1972, p. 11):

Too much of this money has gone into poorly conceived projects, too few of the results have been rigorously assessed, and our means of disseminating the worthwhile results have been too feeble. This means that we know less than we should, that we're less sure of what we know, and that too few people share the knowledge we do possess.

One of Richardson's early acts at HEW was to have the planning and evaluation staff review HEW-supported social R&D and identify tested ideas that were awaiting adoption and promotion. Although a few ideas were identified, the staff concluded, contrary to Richardson's expectations, that "(1) There probably are no hidden jewels coming out of our

R&D that are waiting to be discovered if we just look enough, and (2) if such jewels do exist, our [R&D] bureaus are not apt to find them given the present reporting procedures." (For additional discussion of HEW's efforts to improve the relevance of its social R&D, see "The Question of Relevance" by Laurence E. Lynn, Jr., in this volume.)

Criticism of social R&D sponsored by the Department of Defense was recorded in a report by the National Research Council (1971), which stated (p. 31):

High-level officials, both in the Department of Defense and in the former Bureau of the Budget, believe that research should be more useful to them than it is. Non-mission-oriented basic research is considered to have lacked policy pay-offs and to have constituted both a subsidy to producers and a source of difficulty and irritation with the Congress. Research producers are sometimes viewed as being more interested in furthering their academic disciplines than providing operational help to the Department of Defense.

After surveying a large number of government officials and social scientists, the author of a 1972 article in *Fortune* magazine (Alexander, p. 132) reported that "no one in government is much tempted by the fruits on social science's tree of knowledge."

In 1974, the Nixon Administration's rationale (U.S. Office of Management and Budget 1973) for support of federal research and development programs stressed the importance of recognizing that "how we spend our resources for research and development is just as important as how much we spend" and placed emphasis on "encouraging the focusing of research and development on specific problems within areas of special national need" and on ensuring that "the American people get a proper return on the dollars they invest in federal research and development."

Such concerns have given rise to specific questions: Should the allocation of social R&D resources among social problem areas be changed? Should social R&D funds be spent in different ways? For example, should more be spent on evaluation and experimentation and less on social science research; should more be spent on randomized, controlled field trials and less on uncontrolled demonstrations; should more be spent on research done by universities and research institutions and less on analysis done by profit-making firms; should more be spent on long-term grants and less on short-term contracts? Should the support of social R&D by the federal government be organized and administered differently? For example, should research administration be more centralized; should there be a greater use of formal planning processes; should there be more intramural research; should the potential users of research be more involved in research planning; should there be more interagency coordination?

Executive concern about the usefulness of social R&D is neither surprising nor disturbing. Any federal activity competing for scarce resources will be subjected to critical evaluation by budget examiners, program evaluators, congressional committees, and policy makers. This has been especially true during the chronic budgetary shortages of the early 1970s. Moreover, disillusionment with social R&D has in many respects been a reflection of post-Great Society disillusionment with social programs.

Paradoxically, however, recent insistence by federal officials on relevance and accountability from the research community is a partial reflection of the success the community has had in penetrating government. Following years of urging by social scientists, the policy world now takes it for granted that the social sciences have a contribution to make in government. Policy makers have come to depend on "social engineers" or "research brokers" to communicate expert knowledge. As assistant secretaries, deputy assistant secretaries, and deputy under secretaries for research and program development, research brokers are now a fixture in virtually every federal agency. Professors and researchers from the social science community are regularly appointed to cabinet posts. The staffs of numerous government bureaus and congressional offices have been "upgraded" by the addition of younger members with graduate education and the ability to read, criticize, and evaluate research reports. Through the Congressional Budget Office, the General Accounting Office, the Congressional Research Service, and the Office of Technology Assessment, Congress is developing its own institutionalized cadre of trained policy analysts and social scientists.

These research brokers often exert pressure on the social R&D community to produce results relevant to policy making.[1] Moreover, now that analysts and social scientists are a permanent part of the government, it is unlikely that insistence on relevance will ever abate. In fact, it is likely to increase at all the "right" times, i.e., when knowledge is most needed to clarify complex policy choices. Thus, it would be a mistake to regard the pressure for relevance as aberrant or transitory.

---

[1] In a recent study of social science use, Caplan *et al*. (1975) noted: "The notion that more and better contact [between social scientists and policy makers] may result in improved understanding and greater utilization may be true, but there are also conditions where familiarity may breed contempt rather than admiration."

EFFECTIVE R&D MANAGEMENT

The pressure for relevance is more than just talk. It has taken the form of: increasing reliance in many agencies on competitively awarded contracts (and on sole-source contracts with favored performers) instead of grants, and on grant arrangements that involve collaboration between grantor and grantee; pressures from policy, management, and budget personnel to improve contract and grant administration and research monitoring, dissemination, and utilization; increasing opposition to the use of peer review panels and advisory councils oriented to the research community; and a growing popularity for the forms of social R&D that seem most immediately useful to policy makers— program evaluation, policy analysis, expert consultation, and social experimentation—relative to traditional social science research performed at universities.

In addition, some agencies are experimenting with systematic methods for planning and setting priorities for their social R&D activities (see, for example, Guttentag and Snapper 1974). Occasionally, other management devices have been tried, including policy implications papers prepared in conjunction with completed research projects and the appointment of research consumers to research advisory committees.

Unfortunately, we lack systematic evidence as to whether these steps are having the results their sponsors hope for. There are indications, however, that dissatisfaction with the usefulness of social R&D is not abating. For example, the Federal Council for Science and Technology Task Group on Social R&D noted that there are indications that too little social R&D is relevant to policy making and that too much research, even if relevant, is not available to and utilized by the appropriate decision makers. A 1976 National Research Council review of the National Science Foundation's applied social science research concluded (p. 71): "the quality of the work is highly variable and on average relatively undistinguished, with only modest potential for useful application." In general, social R&D continues to be criticized by members of Congress, executive-branch officials, and social scientists because it is neither good nor well-managed research and has little potential for use.

Although this continued criticism reflects the persistence of the problems that led to criticism in the first place, many in the social R&D community believe that recent pressures for policy relevance have actually been counterproductive. In their view, the attempt to manufacture socially useful knowledge to order—to treat the acquisition of knowledge like any other government procurement—has flooded the market with shoddy products. The resulting poor-quality research, nonreplicable demonstrations, ambiguous experiments, useless data, and biased evaluations have neither policy value nor scientific merit. In the view of others, nothing has changed but the name of the game. For example, one psychologist strongly committed to socially useful research notes (Deutsch 1976, p. 2): "paradoxically, when funding agencies under the edicts of conservative federal administrations have pressured for relevance, the effect has often been just the opposite from that which was intended—an increase occurred only in pseudo-relevancy and much rewriting of project proposals to use the 'relevance' terminology took place." The management skill, financial and manpower resources, and continuity of effort needed to orient the social R&D community more toward the productive study of social problems have been lacking.

This unsatisfactory state of affairs has stimulated still more ideas for reforming social R&D management. One idea is to tighten the management of social R&D still further by centralizing its administration, restricting federal funding mainly to high-priority subjects and projects, subjecting individual project proposals to greater scrutiny, and weakening or eliminating peer review and what is asserted to be its parochial emphasis on methodology and performer reputation (see Gustafson 1975). At the other extreme, some would abandon altogether direct approaches to achieving policy relevance and return the making of social R&D policy to the scientific community. Those holding this view would strengthen, not weaken, peer review and leave the choice of subjects for research, the selection of research methods and performers, and decisions to disseminate research findings to those with scientific qualifications. By thus promoting quality and scientific merit, it is argued, the government would enhance the social usefulness of social R&D in the most fundamental sense.

THE EXTENT OF OUR KNOWLEDGE

In the face of such divergent views, it seems wise to pause and take stock. What knowledge do we possess that is relevant to the formulation of social R&D policy? To what extent and in what manner is knowledge used in resolving social policy problems? By what strategies can the most useful forms of knowledge be obtained?

Regrettably (and ironically), we possess little knowledge obtained through research that will help answer these questions. As Albert Biderman has noted (1970, p. 1067): ". . . social scientists . . . are only slightly more predisposed to rate social scientific knowledge about their business as one of their most critical needs than are people in those social endeavors that social scientists seek a mandate to inform.'' Most studies addressing federal social R&D policy have been promotional, i.e., preoccupied with the extent of federal financial support of social sciences at academic institutions and with the number of social scientists influential in government. Though there is a growing body of social science research on organizational behavior and change, the diffusion of innovations, and the nature of bureaucratic decision making, this research has seldom influenced main arguments or recommendations.

There is recent evidence that this situation may be changing. A study by Caplan *et al.* (1975) helps fill in the large gaps in our understanding of how the use of social science information influences federal government policy. The National Institute of Mental Health has initiated several studies aimed at understanding policy-making processes and the role of social R&D institutions in shaping them. The National Academy of Sciences published *Knowledge and Policy in Manpower*, a landmark study of the manpower research and development program in the Department of Labor (National Research Council 1975). In a study sponsored by the Commission on the Organization of the Government for the Conduct of Foreign Policy (1975), Alexander L. George analyzed the entire body of social science knowledge on decision making and developed ideas on how those making foreign policy decisions could make better use of information.[2]

THE STUDY PROJECT ON SOCIAL R&D

Despite these efforts, the Study Project on Social R&D began its work against a background of generally inadequate knowledge. One thing in particular was apparent. Few of the proposed solutions to the "relevance problem" have been based on a clear conception of what the terms "relevant to policy" or "socially useful" mean.

[2] Though not addressed to the problems of managing social R&D, a recent study of federal biomedical research (Comroe and Dripps 1976) is of considerable methodological interest. "Our project had only one goal," state the authors (p. 105): "to demonstrate that objective, scientific techniques—instead of the present anecdotal approach—can be used to design and justify a national biomedical research policy." Through a rather rigorous empirical process, their study identified what they believed to be the types of research that underlay the top ten clinical advances in cardiovascular and pulmonary medicine and surgery in the last 30 years.

To stimulate thinking about the impact of social R&D on policy, the Study Project asked several persons familiar with both policy making and social R&D to address themselves to questions concerning the relationship between knowledge and policy making:

• *At what times and under what circumstances during the life cycle of a policy or program are the results of social R&D—or, more generally, ideas, analyses, and research findings—likely to be influential in shaping the thinking or motivating the actions of some key participant in the decision-making process? In other words, from the time that public discussion of an issue begins to the time that a program has been operational long enough for its continuation to be questioned, when are research findings likely to matter most?*

• *By what avenues do the results of social R&D affect public policy, e.g., through program managers, the courts, congressional authorizing committees, the educational system, organized interest groups, and public opinion— or through the recruitment of experts into key jobs, internal advocacy, or other means? All of these avenues are used at various times, but are some avenues likely to be more reliable than others? Does it depend on the stage at any given moment of the policy development process? Does it depend on the type of policy being considered? Or what?*

• *In the light of past experience, what criteria or general considerations should be employed in planning social R&D? For example, should the priorities and direction be left largely up to the academic research community, with research managers considering only the quality of the proposal and the reputation of the principal investigator? Or, at the other extreme, should federal policy planners and research managers jointly define in advance the desired research and its relationship to specific policy decisions? Is more or less direction desirable? Should researchers have a constituency in mind? Should users be included in the research planning process? In other words, depending on when, how, and with whom research is likely to be influential, how could federal agencies improve the influence of social R&D on policy?*

In answer to these questions, Carol H. Weiss, James Q. Wilson, Howard R. Davis and Susan E. Salasin, and James L. Sundquist joined me in examining the process of knowledge into policy. Our different views comprise the remainder of this volume. In addition, Sharon M. Collins looked at how social R&D has been used in decision making by the courts, a subject of growing importance.

A COMPENDIUM OF VIEWS

My views have been shaped by having worked in several federal agencies that support social R&D as well as by participation in the Study Project on Social R&D. I believe that federally supported social R&D cannot be fairly judged by any single yardstick of relevance. Because social R&D fulfills many different functions in our pluralistic society, many criteria must be considered when determining whether or not social R&D has been worthwhile. For the most part, assessing usefulness project by project is a mistake. Such an approach to social R&D management will produce too much superficial, secondary-source research and too little investment in theory, methodology, innovative applications, and primary data.

Conceding the existence of problems with the link between social research and public policy, Weiss explores at length the cognitive and structural difficulties associated with the stages of policy research at which the problems are most severe: formulating research and applying research results to policy. She observes that the most commonly proposed solutions to research-into-policy problems are administrative remedies involving tighter control by federal staff. Though some of these remedies may help, in general they have little real impact on the cognitive or structural causes of these problems. Noting that "a democratic system does not want technocratic solutions imposed on decision makers; a pluralistic society does not want political controls on the freedom of research," she counsels that we avoid the "social engineering" concept of social R&D in favor of an "enlightenment" model that views social R&D not as a solution to problems, but as an intellectual backdrop of concepts, propositions, orientations, and empirical generalizations for the discussion of policy.

Basing his observations on personal experiences with a series of governmental commissions and public agencies, Wilson's conclusions are negative: "Public commissions, on the record, have either made no use of social science, . . . made some use but in ways irrelevant to its policy conclusions, . . . or made use of relevant but unconvincing and inadequate research. . . ." Further, "good social science will rarely be used by government agencies in a timely and effective manner. Most organizations change only when they must, which is to say, when time and money are in short supply. Therefore, most organizations will not do serious research and experimentation in advance. When they use social science at all, it will be on an ad hoc, improvised, quick-and-dirty basis." His solution is "not good research, but wise, farseeing, shrewd, and organizationally effective administrators."

Davis and Salasin, too, cite problems with the knowledge-into-policy process from the perspectives of both policy makers and researchers. They develop several suggestions that they believe might improve this process: additional research that will clarify the complexities of policy decision making in ways that will enable researchers better to understand policy makers' needs and problems, closer coordination among social R&D administrators in federal agencies, more flexible and imaginative uses of funding mechanisms, improved quality control, more encouragement of high-performance researchers, and design of and support for effective dissemination media.

Sundquist sees the flow of knowledge into policy taking place via a transmission belt consisting of researchers, academic middlemen, research brokers, and policy makers. Although breakdowns can occur at any point, problems most often arise at the point where a research broker—a staff assistant to a policy maker who can translate social knowledge into policy advice—is needed. Following an analysis of the functions, opportunities, and pitfalls of research brokerage at the federal level, Sundquist suggests that research brokerage may constitute a new discipline, whose practitioners have "a sophisticated understanding of the importance of maintaining a flow of facts and interpretation from the world of research to the world of action and a flow of leadership and support back again. . . ."

Collins surveys the courts' use of four types of social research data (expert testimony, results of existing studies, public opinion polls, and results of studies conducted specifically for the case at hand) from five research sources (economics research statistical data, public opinion surveys, psychological research, and socio-psychological research) in four types of application (criminal law, surveillance, pornography/obscenity, and separation of church and state). Noting that social science research is not uniformly accepted by the legal community, she suggests that the lawyer's faith in research depends on four factors: quantifiability, relevance, the perceived absence of value judgments, and concern for the individual. "This concern is the major dividing force between social scientists and lawyers: while social scientists may criticize the narrow scope of law, lawyers, with matching intensity, mistrust the generalities of social science."

REFERENCES

Alexander, T. (1972) The social engineers' retreat under fire. *Fortune* 86(October):132–36ff.

Archibald, K. (1967) Federal interest and investment in social science. Page 328 in U.S.

House of Representatives, *The Use of Social Research in Federal Domestic Programs.* Part I. Committee on Government Operations. 90th Congress, 1st Session. Washington, D.C.: U.S. Government Printing Office.

Biderman, A. D. (1970) Self-Portrayal. *Science* (350)1064–67.

Caplan, N., Morrison, A., and Stambaugh, R. J. (1975) *The Use of Social Science Knowledge in Policy Decisions at the National Level: A Report to Respondents.* Center for Research on Utilization of Scientific Knowledge. Ann Arbor: University of Michigan, Institute for Social Research.

Comroe, J. H., Jr., and Dripps, R. D. (1976) Scientific basis for the support of biomedical science. *Science* 192(4235):105–11.

Deutsch, M. (1976) On making social psychology more useful. Social Science Research Council *Items* 30(1):1–6.

Gustafson, T. (1975) The controversy over peer review. *Science* 190(4219):1060–66.

Guttentag, M., and Snapper, K. (1974) Plans, evaluations, and decisions. *Evaluation* 2(1):58–74.

National Research Council (1968) *The Behavioral Sciences and the Federal Government.* Washington, D.C.: National Science Foundation.

National Research Council (1969) *The Behavioral and Social Sciences: Outlook and Needs.* Washington, D.C.: National Academy of Sciences.

National Research Council (1971) *Behavioral and Social Sciences Research in the Department of Defense: A Framework for Management.* Advisory Committee on the Behavioral Science Research in the Department of Defense. Washington, D.C.: National Academy of Sciences.

National Research Council (1975) *Knowledge and Policy in Manpower: A Study of the Manpower Research and Development Program in the Department of Labor.* Committee on Department of Labor Manpower Research and Development, Assembly of Behavioral and Social Sciences. Washington, D.C.: National Academy of Sciences.

National Research Council (1976) *Social and Behavioral Science Programs in the National Science Foundation.* Assembly of Behavioral and Social Sciences. Washington, D.C.: National Academy of Sciences.

National Science Foundation (1969) *Knowledge into Action: Improving the Nation's Use of the Social Sciences.* Washington, D.C.: National Science Foundation.

President's Science Advisory Committee (1962) *Strengthening the Behavioral Sciences.* Washington, D.C.: U.S. Government Printing Office.

U.S. Commission on the Organization of the Government for the Conduct of Foreign Policy (1975) *Appendix D: The Use of Information.* Washington, D.C.: U.S. Government Printing Office.

U.S. Congress, House (1967) *The Use of Social Research in Federal Domestic Programs.* 4 vols. Committee on Government Operations. 90th Congress, 1st Session. Washington, D.C.: U.S. Government Printing Office.

U.S. Department of Health, Education, and Welfare (1972) *Responsibility and Responsiveness.* DHEW Pub. No. (OS)72-19. Washington, D.C.: Department of Health, Education, and Welfare.

U.S. Office of Management and Budget (1973) *Special Analyses: Budget of the United States Government.* Fiscal Year 1974. Washington, D.C.: U.S. Government Printing Office.

The Question
of Relevance

LAURENCE E. LYNN, JR.

Historians of science have noted the Enlightenment-influenced, empirically minded spirit in which the nation was founded. Of Washington, Jefferson, and Franklin, Price writes (1954, p. 4): "The first effect of their leadership was to destroy the traditional theory of hereditary sovereignty, and to substitute the idea that the people had the right, by rational and experimental processes, to build their governmental institutions to suit themselves." Lyons adds (1969, pp. 2–3) that the scientific spirit of the founding fathers "was also shaped by a pragmatism and utilitarianism that grew out of the practical demands of settling a new land and that have characterized American society and American science from the beginning."

As President, Thomas Jefferson was responsible for what may have been the first major federally supported social research. ". . . [Perhaps] the most important fact about the Lewis and Clark expedition . . . is the degree to which it was 'programmed,' or planned in advance, down to the smallest detail by Jefferson and his scientific associates in Philadelphia. . . ." (Goetzman 1966, p. 5). In Goetzman's view, the Lewis and Clark expedition could reasonably be construed, at least in part, as basic, as opposed to applied, social R&D (p. 5): ". . . Lewis and Clark might almost be considered a logical extension of the

Laurence E Lynn, Jr., Professor of Public Policy at Harvard University's John F. Kennedy School of Government, has directed policy analysis activities as assistant secretary in several federal agencies.

American Philosophical Society, which existed to promote the general advancement of science and 'the useful arts'." The results, however, were unquestionably in the "applied" category. The expedition "replaced a mass of confusing rumors and conjectures with a body of compact, reliable and believable information on the western half of the continent which caught the imagination of the country" (Dupree 1957, p. 27).

The systematic exploration and survey of the American West in many ways represents a paradigm for the relationship of public policy making and scientific research. In the case of the Lewis and Clark expedition, for example, Jefferson sought relevant, documented knowledge in the face of pressures to act in furtherance of American ambitions in the West but prior to major policy developments. He was systematic in organizing and training an interdisciplinary team to assemble new knowledge on behalf of a broad social goal. "Jefferson's instructions, in their detail, their insistence on astronomical observation, attention to nature history and the Indians, and above all his reiterated admonition to keep every possible record, set a scientific tone for this expedition and for the many that would later copy the pattern he set" (p. 26).

The initiation of this major research enterprise was also accompanied by shrewd, and necessary, political maneuvering: to the Spanish, Jefferson explained his purpose as "the advancement of geography"; to Congress, Jefferson's justification for the expedition was the extension of commerce; his own purposes were diverse and included advancing science, securing intelligence, and laying the basis for diplomacy in the West (p. 26).

It is of further interest to note that events did not obediently wait upon the results of the expedition—the Louisiana Purchase was completed well in advance of widespread dissemination of the expedition's findings. Moreover, dissemination itself was a problem. "The Journals did not apear in any form until 1814, nor in a faithful reproduction until 1904" (p. 28).

Unfortunately, we have no comprehensive, analytic history of the bases for national policy developments and of the role of scientific knowledge and information in shaping these developments. If we did, we might appreciate the general validity of the lessons learned from analyzing the Lewis and Clark expedition: i.e., that Presidential support is necessary to the success of social R&D in affecting national policy; that social research on a significant scale inevitably has multiple, and not necessarily consistent, purposes; that political considerations inevitably shape the research enterprise; that the research needed to solve social problems is a synthesis of many types of knowledge; that a research enterprise needs competent leadership; that events do not wait for research results; and that dissemination is not automatic.

WHAT IS POLICY RELEVANCE?

Many who believe that social R&D ought to be more useful to policy makers base that belief on an idealized view of the policy process.

IN THE BEST OF ALL POSSIBLE WORLDS

Policy makers realize that they have some responsibility for existing social problems. How can we reduce youth crime or curb drug addiction? How can we raise the educational attainment of poor children? How can we enhance productivity and the availability of jobs for the able-bodied unemployed? How can we provide a decent home and a suitable living environment for all Americans? How can we ensure access to health care for the poor and spare all Americans the strains imposed by rapidly rising health care costs? Recognizing such problems, policy makers begin seeking advice and assistance on what to do about them.

Among the sources of advice to policy makers is the social R&D community, comprising the producers of social knowledge. In the best of all possible worlds, this community is continuously and systematically engaged in study of individual, group, institutional, and social behavior. Its members develop models of behavior and empirically test hypotheses derived from these models. Based on their theoretical and empirical studies, they can explain, for example, why people commit crimes or become addicted to drugs, why prices rise while there is substantial unemployment, or what the effects are of unequal educational opportunities.

Furthermore, members of the social R&D community are capable of predicting the consequences of various policy measures that change the incentives facing particular groups and institutions. They can, for example, predict what will happen if the price of natural gas is deregulated, if mandatory sentences are adopted for habitual offenders, if property tax relief is granted to elderly home owners, if mandatory busing is used to achieve school desegregation, and the like. Once they come to understand the policy problem, they can assist in designing policies that will bring about socially desirable behavioral outcomes and in estimating the costs of achieving these outcomes.

They can compare different policies in various terms meaningful to policy makers, such as the effects of different policies on the cost of living, on family stability, on industry profitablity, or on patterns of racial segregation.

Finally the social R&D community may discover social pathology, may identify the extent and causes of poverty, the potential for violence among urban minorities, or the extent of occupationally related mental illness. Thus, the social R&D community will be in a position to provide policy makers with early warnings of potential policy issues and the questions they should be asking.

Even in this ideal world of knowledge-seeking policy makers and knowledgeable social researchers, there would be problems of social R&D management. Through what channels should communications between policy makers and researchers take place? How should the research community be organized and supported while doing its work? When social knowledge is lacking on a problem, when researchers disagree, or when research results are ambiguous, what should policy makers do while additional knowledge or clarification is being acquired? When resources to support social R&D are scarce, how should priorities among research objectives be established?

Moreover, even in ideal circumstances, it is not clear what the indicators of policy-relevant research should be. Research useful to policy makers will probably be the cumulative result of many theoretical, methodological, and empirical investigations. It makes little sense to say that only empirical or applied research is relevant to policy if it depends for its validity on theoretical and methodological work. Nor does it seem sensible to pass judgment on the policy relevance of every individual study. Policy relevance is an attribute of a broad research program in which the accumulated efforts of researchers lead toward useful answers for policy makers. But who is to decide whether a research program is likely to yield useful answers? Who are to be the arbiters of policy relevance, and how will they function?

Thus, even in the best of all possible worlds, managing social R&D for policy relevance would be a difficult task. It becomes more difficult when the complexities of actual policy making are considered.

IN THE REAL WORLD

The Elusive Policy Maker

Who makes income maintenance policy, or crime control policy, or mental health policy? The answer, of course, is that in our system of government there is no single, authoritative policy maker. In the case of most social issues, the power to influence or shape policies and programs is fragmented among the executive branch, the legislature, the judiciary, and organized private interest groups—at all levels of government. Power is further fragmented because of specialization by units in the executive and legislative branches of government; thus, for example, 11 committees of the U.S. House of Representatives, 10 of the U.S. Senate, and 9 executive departments or agencies have some jurisdiction over income maintenance programs.

Participants in policy making have different roles, constituencies, values, interests, perspectives, and abilities. Their attitudes toward research also differ; some value it and some do not. Morever, among those who value it, some are genuinely open-minded in seeking and using research findings, others attempt to mobilize findings for partisan or legitimizing purposes, and still others view research in a tactical, rather than a substantive, context—a research program may be a device for keeping an issue alive or for delaying action.

Policy making that takes place within the framework of an adversary process can hardly be scientific or "rational." Policy decisions are made through bargaining and compromise by participants with widely dissimilar perspectives. If "policy relevance" has any general meaning, it means relevance to the participants in a complex political process. From the point of view of participants, policy-relevant research is research that helps them carry out their roles and achieve goals they consider important.

This situation poses dilemmas for the producers of social knowledge. For a researcher to be relevant in the sense of consciously contributing to a partisan political process may seem incompatible with objective scientific inquiry. Moreover, with so many different participants and perspectives, someone is bound to be dissatisfied and critical concerning the nature and results of virtually any social R&D activity, no matter how useful it may be to a particular participant or how scientifically valid it may be in the eyes of the researcher's peers.

On the other hand, there is abundant evidence that the research community cannot remain aloof or isolated from policy makers and continue to receive federal financial support. Sooner or later, someone—a senator, a budget examiner, or a newly appointed executive—will find it advantageous to ask why continued support of "irrelevant" research is in the agency's, the government's, or the public's interest. Unless the social R&D community has the political muscle to suppress such questions (but are lobbying and special pleading in such a cause compatible with objective science?), some concept of accountability must be developed. The thorny questions of relating knowledge production to a pluralistic political process persist.

Policy: A Moving Target

Policy making is not an event. It is a process that moves through time-consuming stages, beginning with public recognition that a problem exists, to the adoption of laws or a combination of measures aimed at dealing with aspects of the problem (which may take a long time and may never happen), to the establishment and operation of a program, to evaluation, review, and modification—but seldom death.

During the various stages, policy making does not usually wait for relevant knowledge to become available. Under the pressure of events and constituencies, legislation is passed, programs are started, regulations and guidelines are written, and funds are authorized, appropriated, and spent whether or not relevant analysis and research findings are available. Indeed, the process is often reversed: the systematic accumulation of knowledge may not begin until policies and programs are enacted. Once established and in operation, operating programs legitimize the large-scale expenditure of public funds for research. This reversed process has been the case, for example, with issues such as income maintenance, environmental protection, and energy development.

Social problems are seldom "solved" by a single act or policy declaration, even if it seems so at the time. Rather, policies to deal with them are fashioned incrementally over time, in a series of measures that are partial and not necessarily irreversible. In fact, perceptions as to the basic nature of a problem may change as time passes, causing changes in policy. For example, the proper federal role in the financing of health care has been under debate for four decades, and important steps—the Kerr-Mills Act, Medicaid—have been taken. Yet debate continues and further major developments are almost a certainty.

The time-consuming, action-forcing, incremental, and adaptive nature of the policy-making process has several important but conflicting implications for social R&D. First, despite the immediate pressure of events, there is usually time for significant social R&D. While the immediate questions may change over time, the need for research on fundamental issues is a continuing one. Though individual policy makers usually have short time horizons, the policy process has much longer ones, a circumstance hospitable to the time-consuming nature of knowledge production.

Second, however, the farther in the future the research is focused—

the less related it is to immediate issues—and the more remote its usefulness, the smaller its current constituency. Policy making is concerned with current issues and problems. Policy makers would rather commit resources to obtain immediate help than invest in a uncertain future when they may not be around. They will be more impatient with future-oriented research, more likely to cut it back in favor of research that is supposed to have immediate impact.

Third, each incremental step that adds to the complexity of public laws and programs makes future significant action, especially if it involves institutional change, that much more difficult. As time passes and programs evolve, policy making becomes more and more preoccupied with existing programs and institutions and with the vested interests surrounding them. Thus, unless there is a newly emerging policy area, there may be little short-run use of policy ideas derived from research, because policy makers must ultimately contend with the political realities of programs, laws, and the organized interests that support them, with striking bargains rather than with introducing innovations.

The dilemma for social R&D managers or researchers interested in policy relevance is clear. They can invest in the future by supporting basic research, which usually has little current interest but the possibility of significant long-run payoffs, or they can meet their client's near-term needs with research that has more current interest but perhaps more questionable prospect of being of long-term value. Should they concentrate on questions and problems that may be of little current interest and thus have limited and unstable funding, or should they deal with the familiar agenda of social problems for which approval and funds for research are easier to obtain? It is a precarious existence.

THE PROBLEM OF CRITERIA

In this complex world of policy making, what would a policy-relevant research program look like? By what criteria of policy relevance might social R&D be judged? As an example of how this problem might be approached, one could pose several questions with respect to a particular social R&D project:

(1) Have the findings of this study been incorporated into policy?

(2) Have the findings of this study been analyzed and discussed by someone influential in the policy process?

(3) Are the findings of this study potentially relevant to a current policy debate?

(4) Are the findings of this study potentially relevant to future policy debates?

(5) Has this study shed light on the nature of a social problem or condition or on how society or people function?

(6) Has this study contributed to the formulation, design, and conduct of other research projects, the findings of which will be helpful in the making of current or future policy?

(7) Does this study advance an intellectual discipline in a way that will enhance the social usefulness of research conducted within that discipline's framework?

(8) Does this study have scientific merit in the opinion of qualified social scientists?

The choice of criteria will depend on one's values and perceptions concerning the appropriate federal role in supporting social R&D. These perceptions will in turn be influenced by one's specific obligations and responsibilities. For example, if agency R&D managers can answer "yes" to questions (5) through (8), they may argue that all their social R&D projects are relevant to policy. The parent department's management personnel are likely to have more "result-oriented" criteria; research is relevant to policy only if they can answer yes to questions (1) and (2). Members of the department's policy analysis staff, who are likely to have a broader substantive orientation than management personnel but be less "academic" than research managers, may regard research as relevant to policy if they can answer yes to questions (3) and (4). And an academic social scientist might judge all projects for which the answer to (8) is "yes" to be "socially useful," and therefore worthy of federal support. These views represent distinct philosophies of evaluation, and each has merit, particularly in the context of allocating scarce resources.

In addition to the above list and varying views, there are other factors that complicate the choosing of criteria of policy relevance. For example, the initiation of research may represent a holding or delaying action in the political process; it may be a symbolic act, signaling concern or adumbrating future actions; it may be a way for an executive or legislator to placate or support a colleague who needs to show that "something is being done" about a problem. In these circumstances, it may matter less that research is producing useful results than that research is being done at all.

Is research launched for these reasons to be judged irrelevant? Some believe so. Noble, for example, advocating a new, more rigorous system of peer review, argues (1974, p. 920):

> Most important would be the effect that a new system might have by unmasking and curtailing the use of scarce R&D funds for service subsidy and the seeking of influence. . . . [P]rojects serving mixed purposes create ambiguity and, because of the servicing requirements they impose, distract and dissipate the energies of technically qualified R&D administrators. . . .

Whatever the merits of this view, it ignores the realities governing federal support for social R&D. Research activities of various kinds will continue to be initiated for reasons that are branded "political" by scientists. Overseeing such activities with appropriate diligence may be the price researchers must pay for the discretion to conduct research more in line with their interests. The suggestion here, however, is that the social R&D community as well as federal research managers might go beyond merely putting up with "political research" and recognize its legitimacy in the policy-making process, not to mention making the most of such opportunities to learn something useful.

Unfortunately, there are other complications. The act of choosing and applying criteria of policy relevance is itself subject to political and bureaucratic pressures. An example from my own experience illustrates the problem.

In 1972, officials from the Department of Health, Education, and Welfare's Planning and Evaluation Office, the Social Security Administration, the Department of Labor, and the Office of Economic Opportunity began meeting to agree on a design for evaluating the Family Assistance Program, the enactment of which was thought to be a good possibility. All agreed that the evaluation research should produce knowledge useful for income maintenance policy makers. But what knowledge? At the time, the administration's official goal for welfare reform was simply the reduction of welfare rolls; there was hostility in the Office of Management and Budget (OMB), the White House, and elsewhere to intrusive and expensive data collection for research purposes. This climate created problems for researchers who believed the policy-relevant knowledge included evidence about work effort, family stability, consumption, and self-esteem collected from an appropriate sample on a longitudinal basis. Moreover, issues such as these mattered a great deal to some agencies and not at all to others. Though the group included many competent researchers, scientific issues had to compete for attention with bureaucratic and political ones.

Similarly, a recent attempt by OMB to improve the relevance of evaluation research findings to program decision making by including an evaluation plan and the specification of objectives in all legislation brought worried reactions from many agency officials. They rightly perceived that deciding what knowledge is relevant to policy making is a political as well as a scientific judgment. To act as if policy making is scientifically rational when it is not risked saddling research managers with wholly inappropriate objectives and constraints (see Salasin and Kivens 1975, pp. 37–41).

CONCLUSION

With so many dimensions to policy relevance, it might seem that anything goes: a plausible justification can be advanced for virtually any current research project, demonstration, or experiment if "political projects" are permitted. What, then, is the problem?

The problem, as it emerges from studies of federal social R&D management, is twofold: first, few, if any, criteria of relevance are applied during the planning of social R&D. Too little thought is given to the types of knowledge that will be most useful to the agency, to Congress, to third parties, or to supporting disciplines prior to the commissioning of research projects. Little attention is given to developing priorities for guiding project selection. Second, research management typically focuses on individual projects—in fact on each year's "new starts"—rather than on multiyear, multiproject research programs; only infrequently are research projects part of an overall effort to gain knowledge for explicitly stated reasons. This type of management virtually precludes the use of criteria that stress the cumulative and reinforcing effects of research.

Thus, federally supported social R&D seldom seems to add up to anything because it simply was not intended to add up to anything. Ad hoc, ex post rationalizations are rarely adequate to justify—especially in the eyes of skeptical policy making and management officials—research activities that lack a strong and well thought-out a priori rationale.

Ironically, the unsatisfactory outcomes of this type of research management often lead to administrative actions that make matters worse. Attempts are made to tighten individual project management and to apply specific, utilitarian criteria and strict deadlines to each one. Because valuable new knowledge is usually obtained through a cumulative, iterative, time-consuming, and often inefficient process of investigation, the results of applying such procurement methods to knowledge production may deepen the disillusionment with social R&D.

If this analysis is correct, the solution to the relevance problem will have two aspects. First, officials involved in social R&D activities must recognize the complexities of the knowledge-into-policy process and the central insight that follows from it—that many criteria are appropriate to assessing the relevance of social R&D to policy making. Second, criteria of relevance must be consciously applied in the formulation of social R&D agendas, before projects are selected and funded, if social R&D activities are to have coherence and purpose.

Successful implementation of such a solution will require relatively sophisticated oversight and management of social R&D. It is admittedly a difficult task, especially because it almost certainly cannot be imposed by fiat on a set of activities that are necessarily decentralized, diverse, and uncoordinated. If social R&D is to surmount the criticism it continues to receive and if investments in the production and utilization of useful social knowledge are to yield the desired results, it is a solution that those concerned with the health of the social R&D enterprise are well advised to pursue.

REFERENCES

Dupree, A. H. (1957) *Science in the Federal Government: A History of Policies and Activities to 1940.* Cambridge, Mass.: Harvard University Press-Belknap Press.

Goetzman, W. E. (1966) *Exploration and Empire: The Explorer and the Scientist in the Winning of the American West.* New York: Vintage Books.

Lyons, G. M. (1969) *The Uneasy Partnership: Social Science and the Federal Government in the Twentieth Century.* New York: Russel Sage.

Noble, J. H., Jr. (1974) Peer review: quality control of applied social science. *Science* 185(September 13):920.

Price, D. K. (1954) *Government and Science: The Dynamic Relation in American Democracy.* New York: New York University Press.

Salasin, S., and Kivens, L. (1975) Fostering federal program evaluation: a current OMB objective. *Evaluation* 2(2):37–41.

Improving the
Linkage Between
Social Research and
Public Policy

CAROL H. WEISS

INTRODUCTION

Much has been said and written about the limited impact that social research has had on government decisions. Three blue-ribbon commissions, composed largely of social scientists, have reviewed the state of the social sciences in the past decade; all reviewed the use of the social sciences and declared a need for improvement.[1] There have been congressional hearings by a subcommittee of the House Committee on Government Operations (U.S. Congress, House 1967) and an outpouring of books and papers on the subject.[2] The work of the Study Project on Social Research and Development, of which this paper is a part, is another attempt to clarify the relevance of social research.

Neither the topic nor the concern is new. Triggered by the Great Depression and the international crises of the 1930s, sociologist Robert

Carol H. Weiss, Senior Research Associate at the Bureau of Applied Social Research, Columbia University, is the author of numerous books and articles on program evaluation research and the uses of social R&D in policy making. This paper was prepared for the Study Project on Social Research and Development in August 1975.

[1] The Brim Commission was oriented almost exclusively to utilization (National Science Foundation 1968); the Young Committee report is cited as National Research Council (1968); the BASS Committee report is cited as National Research Council (1969).

[2] The title of Irving Louis Horowitz's collection (1971), for example, is graphic: *The Use and Abuse of Social Science*. Other interesting commentaries include: Orlans (1969), Williams (1971), Cowhig (1971), Chinitz (1972), and Roberts (1974).

S. Lynd published the classic *Knowledge for What?* in 1939, and there have been exhortations to social scientists to become more responsive to social needs both before and since.[3] The level of current dissatisfaction is high, but whether it is higher than usual is hard to tell.

There is perhaps some special poignancy to the dissatisfaction because of the sense that the great social programs of the 1960s have failed—or at least fell far short of expectations. A new burst of ideas and inspiration from the social sciences would be a refreshing entry on the political scene. On another plane, there is anxiety over the rumblings emerging from the Congress about the irrelevance of much social science research to government concerns. Government-funded studies with esoteric, silly, or excessively academic titles are ridiculed in public. The House of Representatives went so far as to pass the Bauman amendment, giving Congress a veto over individual research grants made by the National Science Foundation (NSF). (It failed to pass the Senate.) These angry gestures, and the widespread publicity given to Senator Proxmire's attacks on specific social science studies, indicate a level of discontent that appears to some observers an ominous portent of reductions in social science support. To others, the noise seems more a mixture of irritability and grandstanding and a continuation of the Congress's longstanding ambivalence about basic social research.

But with or without the criticisms of sages and yahoos, social scientists have long been concerned about the uses of their work. They are articulate in criticizing the performance of both the social sciences and the government policy-making system and writing tracts about the fit between the two.[4] They have several sources of concern, and, because they tend to play leading roles in diagnosis and prescription for the linkage between research and policy, their concerns are relevant to our analysis.

---

[3] The social science tradition is deeply embedded in social action and social reform. The use of social research for policy purposes goes back at least 200 years. John Howard gathered facts and figures from prisons and prisoners in his drive to reform English prison management in the 1700s. Frederic Le Play (1806–1882) studied family budgets of the European working class not only because of scientific interests but also as a basis for practical proposals for social amelioration. Charles Booth's study of poverty among London working classes in the late 1880s had a decisive effect on English poor relief. In the United States, the Pittsburgh Survey, which began in 1909, examined the conditions of industrial workers and analyzed effects on the community with rapid industrial expansion and was responsible for much urban reform (Young et al. 1939).

[4] Of course, there are many academics who do not see a role for social science in service to the welfare-warfare state. Research that serves as handmaiden to those in power is a violation of the essentially critical role of the scientist (see Gouldner 1970, Dye 1972).

In the first place, social scientists tend to believe in rationality. They have convictions that the best knowledge available should be used in the making of the policy: that when good theory and good data are placed at the service of policy makers, the subsequent decisions will be sounder and wiser. They believe that social science research can improve understanding of the complex interrelationships of social processes, and, in the doing, it can increase the rationality of decision making.

Entangled with this lofty conviction are some more self-serving motives. If key policy makers take social science into account, then the social sciences matter. The social science career is vindicated. The standing of the social sciences is higher and the rewards and recognition available to the individual are greater. The grants economy on which many social researchers are dependent will flourish, and NSF, the National Institute of Education, and the National Institutes of Health and their kin will keep growing and dispensing largesse to the worthy.

Further, social researchers can affect public policy. They are no longer restricted to the small world of the campus but have an influence on important happenings. The papers and reports that they write need not find their final resting place in other researchers' footnotes but are valued by important people in real-world activities. They and their work can make a difference in health care or education or environmental control.

Finally, there is the potential for nudging policy in the direction in which they believe. Social scientists tend to cluster on the left-liberal end of the political spectrum. The Carnegie study of 60,000 faculty members (Lipset and Ladd 1972) indicated that in colleges and universities, which are relatively liberal places to begin with, the most liberal groups on campus are sociologists, social workers, anthropologists, political scientists, and psychologists. While 41 percent of all faculty scored very liberal or liberal on the liberalism-conservatism scale, the equivalent percentage for all social scientists was 63 percent; for sociologists, 72 percent; anthropologists, 64 percent; psychologists, 62 percent; political scientists, 61 percent; and economists, 57 percent.[5] The interests of social scientists in policy to some degree reflect their political convictions. Some of them see the use of objective research evidence as a means to minimize the influence of special interests on public policy, to counteract the lobby, the pressure group, the special pleader, the trade association or large corporation, the politicians who

[5] Confirming evidence on this point can be found in Orlans (1973).

trade favors rather than act in the public interest. Social science, in this view, will advance the common weal by giving voice to the underdog, the deprived, the groups who have no advocate of their own in councils of power. Through social research, social scientists can help to redress the balance of power, tipped too far right by the constellation of power and wealth, reconstruct social institutions, and help move the country toward greater equality.

Thus, social scientists' concern about improving the utility of social research rests on a rational belief in the potential of social science as a guide to policy. It may be buttressed by (1) interest in the status and rewards that accrue to the social science disciplines, (2) desire for influence in the corridors of power, and/or (3) reformist zeal to move public policy in the direction of their own beliefs, usually liberalism and equality.

This excursion into possible motives of social researchers may look like a byway, but to the extent that the speculations are true, they suggest that the vantage point for much analysis on this issue is not completely disinterested. People's motives and interests help to shape their perception of the problem. Social scientists tend to start out with the question: how can we increase the use of research in decision making? They assume that greater use leads to improvement in decisions. Decision makers might phrase it differently: how can we make wiser decisions, and to what extent, in what ways, and under what conditions, can social research help? These are not the same question.

NATURE OF THE PROBLEM

How serious is the mismatch between the knowledge needs of decision makers and the research results of social scientists? Is social research really neglected? Before we try to clarify the nature of the problem and propose solutions, it is well to marshal available evidence about whether the problem really exists.

Nathan Caplan and others of the University of Michigan recently conducted an interview study (1975) with 204 federal decision makers about their use of social science research. Only 9 percent of the respondents could not name a single use of social science knowledge on the job. The rest of the respondents gave 575 instances of use. It is acknowledged that many of the cited uses were of social science concepts rather than specific studies, many were relatively low-level uses, and over half of the instances referred to research, statistics, or analysis done within the agency; still, the picture is not nearly as gloomy as the doomsayers had painted it. Caplan finds that research use in government is at least "modest."[6] Moreover, government officials gave high endorsement to social research: 85 percent agreed that the social sciences can contribute a great deal to the formation of intelligent policy, and 87 percent believed that government should make the fullest possible use of social science. This doesn't sound like the wilderness of the social science laments, where researchers toil long and hard in the policy vineyards only to have their work spurned and their reputations tarnished by contact with the antediluvian boors who inhabit government offices.

Still, as closer inspection of these data and much other evidence suggests, there is obvious room for improvement. The prevailing expectations for use of social science knowledge and research are much higher than reported use. There is a sense that specific research studies and sets of studies should provide hard data and solid bases for decisions. The "soft" and indirect use of rather general social science concepts (which accounts for many of Caplan's instances of use) does not satisfy many current definitions of "research utilization."

THE MANY USES OF RESEARCH

A RANGE OF MEANINGS

What is meant by "research utilization"? Many meanings are attached to the term, and much of the sogginess in discuisons of "policy uses of social research" derives from conceptual ambiguities. Upon examination, research use is an extraordinarily complicated phenomenon. Without any attempt at exhaustiveness, eight different meanings can be distinguished.

---

[6] It is an interesting sidelight that Caplan's 1975 conclusions represent some reorientation of his initial reading of the data. The spring 1974 *ISR Newsletter* gave an early report on the study under the headline "Science Is Seldom Put to Good Use by U.S. Officials." The story was not as negative as the headline, but it did quote Caplan as saying that "officials often lack the skills and proper orientation to put scientific knowledge to good use" (vol. 2, no. 2, p. 2). It also cited Caplan's division of government officials into types of users and his conclusion that five out of ten federal officials fall into the "low-usage" types. Apparently, it was through reconceptualizing and recoding what constituted a "use of knowledge" that more favorable conclusions were forthcoming. The reconceptualization subsumed the use of social science concepts, perspectives, and generalizations as well as specific data or research conclusions and, as this discussion will indicate, makes good sense in light of the ways in which social science actually penetrates the policy world.

Research for Problem Solving

When people discuss the use of social research for policy making, the usual meaning involves a direct and instrumental application. Research that is "used" provides empirical evidence or conclusions that help to solve a policy problem. The model is a linear one: a problem exists; information or understanding is needed either to generate a solution to the problem or to select among alternative solutions; research provides the missing knowledge; a solution is reached.[7] Implicit in this model is the assumption of a consensus on goals. It is assumed that both policy makers and researchers tend to agree on what the desired end should be; the contribution of research is to help in the identification and selection of the appropriate means to reach that goal.

The evidence that social research provides for the decision-making process can be qualitative and descriptive, such as rich observational accounts of social conditions or program processes; it can be quantitative data, either on relatively soft indicators (such as public attitudes) or on hard factual matters (such as number of hospital beds); it can be statistical relationships between variables, generalized conclusions about the associations between factors, even relatively abstract theories about cause and effect.

In this formulation of research use, there are two basic ways in which social research can enter the policy-making arena. First, the research can antedate the policy problem and be drawn in on need. Decision makers stumped for an answer can look for information or ideas from preexistent research, or research can be called to their attention by anyone from reseachers to staff analysts to knowledgeable friends and colleagues, or they may happen upon it in newspapers, magazines, professional journals, or agency newsletters. There is an element of chance in this route from research to decision. Available research may not directly fit the problem; finding appropriate research in the library or through computerized information systems may be difficult; inside experts and outside consultants may fail to come up with relevant sources. Whether or not the relevant research reaches the person with the problem depends on the efficiency of the communications links.

A second route is the purposeful commissioning of research to fill a particular knowledge gap. In this case, it is assumed that decision makers have a clear idea of their goals and a map of acceptable alternatives but lack some specific items of understanding. Thereupon,

---

[7] The National Institute of Mental Health (1971) published an annotated bibliography on research utilization that tends to stress this viewpoint.

they engage social researchers to provide data, analytic generalizations, and possibly interpretations of these generalizations to the case in hand by way of recommendations. This process of acquiring social research to order leads to what some observers have called a decision-driven model of research (Figure 1). Research generated in this type of sequence, even more than research located through search procedures, is expected to have direct and immediate applicability and will be used for decision making.

For either of these routes, it is often assumed that one specific study will be used for decision making. Whether located or acquired for the purpose, the single study on the topic of concern—with its data, analysis, and conclusions—is expected to affect the choices of decision makers. In particular, the large-scale, government-contracted policy study, tailored to the specifications set by government staff, is expected to make a difference in plans, programs, and policies.

This is the typical image of the problem-solving use of research, and much of the remainder of this paper is devoted to analyzing the conditions that block this type of use in the world of policy. But there are other kinds of use, too, and it is useful to consider some alternative formulations.

Research Use as a Knowledge-Driven Model

Research is sometimes used for policy making not so much because an issue requires elucidation but because research has uncovered an opportunity that can be capitalized upon. Examples of this model generally come from the physical sciences: biochemical research makes oral contraceptives available; developments in electronics enable television broadcasters to multiply the number of channels. Because of the fruits of basic research, new applications are developed and new policies emerge. This model (Figure 2) is probably the hoariest one in the literature on research use (see, for example, Havelock 1969).

The linear sequence of events shown in Figure 2 assumes that the

FIGURE 1   Decision-driven model of research.

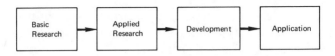

FIGURE 2   Knowledge-driven model of research.

sheer existence of knowledge presses it toward development and use.[8] In social research, however, this is not likely to be the case. Social science knowledge is not apt to be so compelling, nor does it readily lend itself to conversion into technologies, either material or social. Development and application are probably less likely to occur unless a social problem has been consensually defined and politicized and potential solutions debated.

This is by no means to imply that basic research in the social sciences is not useful—even for very practical decisions. Certainly many social policies and programs of government are based, implicitly or explicitly, on basic psychological, sociological, economic, and anthropological research orientations. When they surface to affect government decisions, however, it is not likely to be through the sequence delineated in the knowledge-driven model (Figure 2).

Research Use as an Interactive Model

David Donnison (1972) specifies four fields whose members largely set government policies: politics, technologies, practice, and research (p. 526–27):

Those who are active in each field communicate with those in the others, either directly or through intermediate sections of public opinion. . . . There is no end to the ramifications of the game as the ball is passed back and forth from one field to another.

In his discussion of the British Town and Country Planning Act of 1968, which introduced new procedures, and the Rent Act of 1965, which introduced a new system of rent regulation, Donnison concludes (p. 527):

The relationships between those working in the different fields involved were neither orderly nor linear: they were less like an industrial process than a

---

[8] There is some evidence that even in areas of need in the natural sciences, basic research does not necessarily push toward application. For example, Project Hindsight indicated faster, and probably greater, use of basic science when it was directed toward filling a recognized need in weapons technology (Sherwin *et al.* 1966, Sherwin and Isenson 1967).

market place. In this market place, decisions had to be taken when circumstances—particularly political circumstances—permitted or compelled: it was not feasible to wait, as is inevitable in the case of technological innovations, until the necessary research and development work had been completed. Research workers could not present authoritative findings for others to apply; neither could others commission them to find the "correct" solution to policy problems: they were not that kind of problem. Those in the four fields from which experience had to be brought to bear contributed on equal terms. Each was expert in a few things, ignorant about most things, offered what he could, and generally learnt more than he could teach.

England is a relatively small country, and the close-working relationships that Donnison discusses are probably easier to come by when specialists in the four fields are found within a 50-mile radius, but the model has applicability beyond the face-to-face setting. The use of research becomes part of a complicated process that also uses experience, political insight, pressure, social technologies, and judgment.

Research Use as Conceptualization

Another mode of using research steps back further from an immediate policy issue. Social research can be used in conceptualizing the character of policy issues or even redefining the policy agenda. Thus, social research may sensitize decision makers to new issues and help to turn what were nonproblems or private problems into policy issues, such as child abuse (Weiss 1976). In turn, it may help to convert existing policy issues into nonproblems (e.g., marijuana use). It may drastically revise the way that a society thinks about issues (e.g., acceptable rates of unemployment) and the facets of the issue that are viewed as susceptible to alteration as well as the alternative measures that can be considered.

Global reorientation of this sort is not likely to be the outcome of a single study or even one specific line of inquiry. Over time and with the accumulation of evidence, however, such use can have far-reaching implications. Thus, it is now fairly common to believe that behavior change can precede attitude change rather than follow it. It is accepted that changing the achievement and mobility of poor people is extremely difficult, even with well-meaning social programs; because of their anchoring in personal relationships, they often hold norms and expectations at variance with the middle-class norms of the programs. (A more detailed discussion of "research as enlightenment" appears later.)

The uses of social science research discussed so far can be considered legitimate; that is, they are uses that most social scientists, at least, would agree are "good." There are other ways to use research, however, that seem less acceptable.

Research as Political Ammunition

Very often, the constellation of interests around a policy issue predetermines the positions taken by decision makers. Their opinions are set, and they are not receptive to new evidence. For reasons of ideology, intellect, or interest, they have taken a stand that research evidence is not likely to shake.

In such cases, research can still be used: it becomes ammunition for whichever side finds its conclusions congenial and supportive. Partisans brandish the evidence in an attempt to neutralize opponents, convince waverers, and bolster supporters. Even if conclusions have to be ripped out of context (with suppression of the evidence "on the other hand"), research becomes grist to the partisans' mill.

This kind of activity is a use of research, too; elsewhere (Weiss 1973) I have argued that it is not an unimportant or improper use. To the extent that research adds strength to the position that has objective evidence to support it (without distortion) and to the degree to which research tips the balance toward the "correct" side, it makes a difference—in the right direction.

Research Use as Manipulation

There was a time not so long ago when people worried about the abuse of the social sciences to manipulate and control human behavior, a la Orwell's *1984*: social science harnessed to government authority could be used for thought control, brainwashing, and the subjugation of the human spirit. As 1984 actually approaches, observers tend to be more impressed with the frailties of social science than with its power. Nevertheless, serious attention is currently being paid to "technology assessment" to foretell the possible consequences (primarily the negative consequences) of scientific research and development, and it is possible to envision a similar effort being made to foretell the consequences, particularly the negative consequences, of social research used to manipulate and control human beings.

"Manipulation" may be a word that simply indicates use in ways that contravene the observer's values. In some settings, such as the industrial plant, social science research tends to be devoted to increasing productivity and decreasing absenteeism, without much attention to improving the quality of the work life of the worker. From some perspectives, this is a manipulative use of social science. Similarly, critics of federal social programming point to instances of social science research's being used to blame victims of poverty and injustice (Caplan and Nelson 1973) rather than to alter the social conditions under which such people live in this society. The question of values in social research use is a matter that will be discussed at length.

Research Used to Advance Self-Interest

The list of miscellaneous, more or less self-serving uses of research involves both policy makers and researchers. Social science research can be used by policy decision makers to delay action or to avoid taking responsibility for a decision. It can be used to gain recognition for a successful program—even to win reelection. Skillful use of research can discredit a political opponent or a disliked policy or maintain the prestige of an agency through its support of prestigious researchers. On the other hand, researchers often have their own interests at heart, too: to keep universities and their social science departments solvent, to support faculty and graduate students, to train new social science researchers, and to generate further research on topics that they believe are important. These are all uses—are we willing to say that research is used to the extent that it fulfills functions such as these? Or are some of them ipso facto "illegitimate"? When is a use not a legitimate use? Some value-based criteria have to be invoked.

Finally, we turn to a "use" that seems indistinct and amorphous but that may, in the long run, have weighty implications: social science as a language of discourse (Orlans 1971).

A Language of Discourse

The concepts and theoretical orientations of the social sciences, above and beyond specific research findings, have entered the consciousness of educated Americans, including government decision makers. Ideas, such as externalities, reference groups, political socialization, and intergenerational dependency, have penetrated the corridors of power. There are some currently accepted procedures within government that are at least in part derived from social science approaches: cost-benefit analysis, evaluation, policy analysis, and social experiments. There is emphasis on rational, scientific procedures for development of policy, based in part on the social scientific tradition.

A common language, a mode of discourse, a focusing of an angle of vision on the world—perhaps the common substantive content of that language is the idea of people being shaped by the social context. Although capable of acting and initiating, they are affected in sharp and subtle ways by their recurrent and patterned interactions with others.

DIMENSIONS OF RESEARCH USE

The use of research, then, is an inexact and confused concept. To clarify it, one would have to begin to specify a number of important dimensions:

• What is used—e.g., recommendations or findings from a specific study, findings from a series of related studies, syntheses of research findings on a particular topic, empirical generalizations from studies across topics, social science concepts, social science methods, theoretical orientations.

• By whom it is used—e.g., immediate decision makers, staff members who brief or advise decision makers, administrators who carry out decisions and thereby inevitably modify them, interest groups, line staff, practitioners or clientele who propose new policies or decisions, courts.

• By how many people it is used—is one convinced reader who forcefully propounds the research and advocates a position based on it sufficient, or is some minimal penetration of the decision-making group required?

• How direct the derivation from research is—must someone have read the original report, a summary, or merely a description of the report? How useful is a second- or third-hand account, a popularized version, or someone's recollection that there was "some research on this"?

• How much effect is needed before research is considered "used"—e.g., if the recommendations are implemented in toto; the researchers' interpretations of the findings influence the decision in the direction that research suggests; the interpretations or findings affect the decision but in ways unexpected or peripheral to the research intent; the research is considered but disregarded because of more compelling concerns, such as financial limitations or partisan advantage. (There are actually two dimensions embedded here—the strength of impact and the direction of impact vis-à-vis the researchers' interpretation.)

• How immediate the use is—e.g., considered immediately for the decision at hand, considered for longer-term plans, slowly percolated into orientations toward decisions.

• At what stage in the decision-making sequence use occurs—e.g., recognizing problems, setting agendas, searching for solutions, initiating proposals, assessing alternative proposals, negotiating compromises, selecting a proposal, justifying a decision, implementing a decision, reviewing or revising a decision.

A Definition of Use

For the purposes of this discussion, the common instrumental definition of use will be adopted: if a decision maker considers the findings of a study or a group of related studies for near-term resolution of a policy problem, then that research is being used. The research may not affect the decision, but it does get a fair hearing. In many cases, the competition from other sources of policy advice is so severe that to expect that research will carry the day (or even a portion of the day) is unrealistic.

The policy world is a complicated arena in which previous knowledge and experience abound and each new study has to be fitted into existing views of the world. Moreover, a large number of people, all with their individual theoretical and informational perspectives, are involved in making and implementing any decision, and their differences have to be resolved through the give-and-take of negotiations. There is a plethora of divergent interests, groups with a stake in the policy outcome, groups whose remuneration, reputation, and advancement hinge on an appropriate decision. Policy making, as Lindblom (1965) notes, is not simply removal or substantial reduction of a problem, "but also, and sometimes instead, reconciliation of interests." For these reasons, the opportunities for research to make an impact are circumscribed.

Social scientists often have grandiose expectations, perhaps tainted with self-interest, of the potential effects of social research on policy. While government officials are favorably disposed to social science, they tend to use social science concepts and findings at modest levels. One reason is that the knowledge base in the social sciences is modest, and reliance on it has not been demonstrated to improve the wisdom of public decisions. It may be that the expectations of social scientists are too high, that immediate and direct use is expected when partial and second-order use is reasonable. The passage of social science knowledge through the filter of political judgment may often be a preferable route to action.

Still, the many cases of utter disjunction between knowledge needs and knowledge use require investigation. What will improve the linkage between social science research and policy making? And, in a deeper sense, how can the social sciences most effectively contribute to the wisdom of public policy?

ACTORS IN THE RESEARCH-INTO-POLICY PROCESS

Let us begin the analysis of the process of using social science research to formulate policy with a brief introduction to the major actors: the researcher and the federal policy maker (Figure 3).

Actors in the research-to-policy process are members of different institutional worlds. They respond to the norms of their own institutions, and any attempt to mesh the spheres more closely has to take the varying structural conditions into account.

By definition, researchers in this discussion are social scientists whose government-funded research is expected to contribute to the mission of a federal agency. We are not talking about those engaged in fundamental, discipline-oriented research. The research used in formulating policy decisions can include surveys of conditions, analysis of the interrelationships among variables, evaluations of programs, opinion surveys of relevant people and groups, studies of organizational behavior, etc. It can range from fundamental, theoretically based inquiry to immediately practical analysis of existing data, but, what-

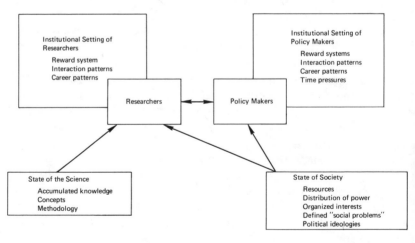

FIGURE 3   Influences on key actors in the research-policy system: researchers and policy makers.

ever the mode of research, there is an expectation of some contribution to policy or program decisions.

Researchers' behavior is strongly influenced by the institutional settings in which they work. If they are faculty members of a university, they respond to the academic reward system. Rewards are based on publishing research results in books and journals and hewing close to the mainline interests of the discipline rather than getting enmeshed in interdisciplinary research, which is often derogated as watered down scholarship. Similarly, they are affected by the interaction patterns in the university—the people they work with and talk to, the meetings they attend. Their career goals, climbing the rungs of the ladder to tenure and full professorship, also help to determine what they are and are not likely to do. This is an oft-told story, which need not be belabored, except to emphasize researchers' response to the knowledge-building and discipline-tending functions of the university.

Policy makers in this discussion are government officials whose positions require them to participate in decisions of substantial scope and cost. They are involved in the planning and formation of policy and programs of national extent and in their adoption, implementation, and administration. They respond to a very different set of institutional arrangements from those that affect researchers. The rewards, interactions, and career patterns in the bureaucracy foster activity and accomplishment, accommodation with other actors, and caution about stepping too far beyond the departmental line. Policy makers have to satisfy their superiors (in the Office of the Secretary, the Office of Management and Budget, or the White House) and consult with a range of interested parties in other executive agencies, the legislature, the agency constituencies, and often state and local governments. The work is geared to a fiscal year, in which annual budgeting and the calendar of expiring legislation create pressures to get decisions made. Legislative policy makers are responsive to the special characteristics of their environment: the pressures of the legislative leadership, their local constituents, and the imperatives of the next election.

Limitations on Actors

There are many factors that limit the activity of both researchers and policy makers. Researchers are affected by the state of their science; its maturity in theory, knowledge, and method sets limits on the authoritativeness of their research. Policy makers and researchers alike are affected by the state of society. One of the important societal inputs to the policy research process is the prevailing definition of social problems, that is, which problems the citizens believe that government should deal with. Furthermore, the range of acceptable social and political ideology sets bounds on the research that can be undertaken and listened to.

Research Funding Agents

In almost every case, there is a third party in the research policy-making process: the research funder (Figure 4). Some people in this category manage research grants programs in mission agencies. Their job is to make known the research interests of the agency and to select from among the applications submitted, usually with the help of peer review panels, the research proposals that the agency will fund.

Other research funding agents sit in offices of planning, analysis, research, and evaluation. They are responsible for obtaining research to meet government needs. They can issue requests for proposals (RFPs) to potential bidders, or occasionally, after thorough demonstration of the researchers' unique qualifications, they can accept an unsolicited proposal under "sole source" procedures. In issuing an RFP, they can specify in great detail which research questions shall be addressed, by what methods, who and how many shall be studied,

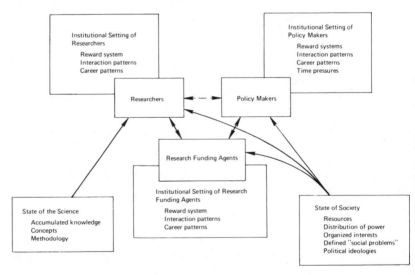

FIGURE 4   Influences on key actors in the research-policy system: research funding agents.

what measures and analytic procedures will be used, down to the outline of the final report—or they can leave considerable latitude for the researcher's judgment. They review proposals, select the research organization with the most appropriate proposal, and fund it by contract for the specific task.

Funding agents, too, respond to the settings in which they work. Their motivations and rewards differ from those of both policy maker and researcher. In some research grants programs, they tend to adopt an academic orientation and view their role as advancing the state of knowledge rather than as aiding policy. In other research offices, they are responsive to the practical pressures of immediate political choices. Particularly when they report directly to policy officials, they can get enmeshed in "fire fighting," handling the emergencies of the moment and trying to use research as a tool in these activities. Still other research funders seek a middle way, stimulating research on topics germane to policy with an emphasis on understanding the dimensions of social problems and the dynamics that sustain them.

When funders fund research, there is an assumption that they will make use of the research when it is completed. At least, it is assumed that they should call it to the attention of those engaged in taking positions and making decisions on the subject. In some offices, this part of the job is perpetually scanted. So much effort goes into research planning, study definition, proposal review, and (sometimes) project monitoring that little time remains for deciding what to do with incoming results. In some cases, funders are ignorant of who needs to know what. They are isolated from significant segments of the policy debate and unaware of which officials need the information and conclusions that are being reported. The report goes into the file, is routed to a third-tier bureau whose interest is dubious, or used as testimony to the funder's own qualifications and performance on the job. Large multiagency departments like the Department of Health, Education, and Welfare (HEW), and research programs dedicated to multiple vaguely specified clients, like the National Science Foundation's Research Applied to National Needs, are probably particularly susceptible to gaps in communication.

The intermediary position that funders occupy between the policy maker and the researcher creates the possibility of distortion in communications, however unintentional. They may misinterpret policy makers' knowledge needs to researchers and, by the same token, may distort research findings to policy makers. If the process is to work better, they are a vital link to be considered.

THE RESEARCH-INTO-POLICY PROCESS AND ITS OBSTACLES

There are three major stages in the policy research process:

- Research Formulation. Questions that research will address are identified. This involves identifying a policy issue and a need for knowledge about the issue; it requires translating the knowledge needs into research questions.
- Conduct of the Study. Data sources are selected, measures developed, samples drawn, and data collected and analyzed.
- Policy Implications. Research results are translated back into the realm of policy. At this stage, the implications of the data for resolution of the policy issue are made explicit, and the results are disseminated to potential users.

In some cases, the policy issue is widely recognized, perhaps already high on the public agenda. Government officials as well as researchers may participate in identifying the facets of the issue that require study and analysis. In other cases, research precedes official or public awareness than an "issue" even exists. The researcher's formulation may serve both to stimulate interest and to shape the definition of the issue as it acquires public visibility.

In either case, a critical phase in research formulation is the specification of concepts and questions. Since no issue can be studied directly and whole, there is a need to select facets of the issue for study, to operationalize the concepts that will be used (e.g., what concretely do we mean by "needs service," "works well," "learning"?) and to determine where and how the research will be carried out.

Although this paper will concentrate on Stages 1 and 3, research formulation and policy implications, the conduct of research, Stage 2, cannot be ignored, for, at the least, it has spillover effects both fore and aft. If appropriate concepts and methodologies are lacking, research cannot be formulated in ways that snugly fit the policy problem. If the research methods used compromise either internal validity or external generalizability of conclusions, the reception of those conclusions in the policy world may well be skeptical.

Coleman has argued (1972) that the conduct of social research lies largely within the domain of the social science disciplines. Whatever goes awry at that stage to lower the quality of research and limit its applicability has to seek a remedy mainly within the disciplines—and of course many things can and do go wrong. Relevant theoretical orientations are often lacking; methods are inadequately developed for some kinds of study; multivariate analytic techniques are in the process of development and not yet suited to cope with certain types of complexities.

Furthermore, not every social scientist functions at the peak standards that current developments permit. Many are mediocre or out-of-date in their research skills. Rather than aspire to apply existing methods creatively to novel problems, they adhere to textbook injuctions. A simple example, but by no means the most important one, is the ritualistic use of 0.05 levels of statistical significance, regardless of the statistical technique, the type of problem, the relative need for certainty, or the real-world risks that accrue to error.

The remedies for such ills have to be sought mainly within the disciplines and their native habitat: the university departments. Universities should be the source of theoretical and conceptual advances and methodological improvements. They also have the responsibility to find better ways of training students in research skills and of upgrading the skills of current researchers, for of course not only policy-oriented researchers but also discipline-oriented researchers are plagued by conceptual and methodological shortcomings. This topic is a large one and worthy of substantial development.

Before we leave the subject of research performance, it is only fair to mention that factors within the policy domain often impinge on research performance. For example, government funding agencies can subvert research quality by mandating inappropriate data sources or research methods or unduly foreshortened time schedules. Data derived from official records or agency files may be inaccurate, out-of-date, incomplete, improperly coded, or irrelevant to key issues. While major responsibility for proper research performance lies within the academic sphere, interactions with the sphere of policy can monumentally affect the quality of the research results.

Given all the concerns about research practice, the problems in formulating research and applying results to policy are even more complex, and they have barely been mapped. It is at the boundaries between the worlds of policy and social science research that analysis and remedy are required.[9]

Two stages of the policy research process involve complex transitions: Stage 1, which concerns the transition from policy issue to research formulation, and Stage 2, which concerns the transition from

[9] For a similar formulation, see Lazarsfeld *et al.* (1967).

research findings to policy implications. The difficulties that plague these phases are of two kinds: (a) intellectual and cognitive and (b) social and structural. The first category of problems has to do with limits on knowledge; the second has to do with the limitations and pressures imposed on actors by the institutions in which they work and the system in which they function.

Figure 5 provides the framework for our analysis of what is going wrong in the development and use of government-funded research:

(1) As we shall note, intellectual limitations affect the specification of research that matches knowledge needs. Cell A contains the cognitive problems involved in formulating policy-related research. In this category, we will discuss such problems as understanding the knowledge needed for developing, adopting, and implementing policies, predicting knowledge needs far enough in advance to plan research, and limitations in the theoretical bases and the methodological apparatus of the social sciences.

(2) The institutional location of policy makers and researchers can give rise to diversion, distraction, and distortion. Cell B deals with social structural limits on research formulation. The social structures that the actors inhabit affect their orientations, their awareness of knowledge needs, and the strategies at their disposal for developing and funding research.

(3) Intellectual limitations impede the interpretation of research results and the development of recommendations for action. Cell C has to do with the translation of data into the realm of policy. We shall look at problems of differing conceptual assumptions and orientations, inconclusive and ambiguous data, and translation from the general to the concrete situation.

Stages of the Policy Research Process	Intellectual/Cognitive Domain	Social/Structural Domain
From Policy Issue to Research Formulation	A Specification of the Research Problem	B Institutional Location of Policy Makers and Researchers
From Research Findings to Policy Implications	C Interpretation of Research Findings	D Application of Research to Policy

FIGURE 5 Sources of difficulty in applying social research to policy.

(4) Cell D deals with structural constraints on the application of research findings to policy making. Problems that we will consider under this rubric include the lack of adequate channels for dissemination of research, political factors that compete with research for attention, and constraints introduced by the complexity of the process by which political decisions are made.

In the following discussion, I have drawn from my own experience, the experience of colleagues, observation, published case histories, and analytical accounts. Many of the points are reinforced by the interview responses of government decision makers and researchers in a study funded by the National Institute of Mental Health on the usability of government-funded research.

SPECIFYING THE RESEARCH PROBLEM

Cognitive Limits

SPECIFYING THE NEEDED INFORMATION Many policy makers find it difficult to specify the nature of the information that would make a difference to their decisions. As one example, a decision maker in the field of alcoholism was asked what kind of research would help him in his work. He specified research on the biological bases of alcoholism. The interviewer handed him an abstract of a study on that topic and asked him how likely he would be to take the study into account in reaching decisions. He read the findings and said: not very likely. Although the findings were interesting, his office had to plan and provide treatment for alcoholism—regardless of its origins. In 15 minutes, he had telescoped a not-uncommon process that usually takes several years, thousands of dollars, and countless units of frustration.

Not only is it hard for decision makers to identify the topics on which research should be done, but it is even harder for them to specify the particular kinds of data or statistical relationships that would clarify an issue. Sometimes they overspecify the research question, assuming more than is known and foreclosing a range of possibilities; they move to the immediate and practical before the shape of the issue is clear. On the other hand, they sometimes overgeneralize the question, offering vague objectives without direction as to the limits on acceptable alternatives or available instrumentalities (Merton and Lerner 1951). Requests for proposals, RFPS, couched in this kind of wide-open form, in which the researcher is given little more than a global objective, have been called "requests for prayers."

If policy makers are unclear about what they expect from research, researchers have to ferret, guess, and improvise. The researcher who is well-versed in the substantive field may do very well indeed; researcher-initiated studies are often exceedingly relevant to decision needs. Even under these conditions, however, the research may not be as effectively applied as it should be; policy makers who do not know what they want are not likely to recognize it when they get it. Therefore, we may hazard the proposition that the less able policy makers are to crystallize their informational needs, the less likely they are to use research effectively.

OFFICES OF RESEARCH EVALUATION   Surrogates for policy makers, such as staff in research, evaluation, or analysis offices, actually initiate much federally sponsored research. Even when they are located within the same agency, however, they sometimes are poorly apprised of decision makers' needs. In their soliciting of research, they may focus on aspects of the issue that are not the crux on which decisions hinge. Research staff tend to be more academic and less political than policy makers, and they may make central to their definition of needed research the abstract goal rather than the practical need (e.g., "improvement in reading achievement" rather than "keeping middle-class children in city public schools"). Also, because of their remove from the arena of decision making, they may stick to official statements rather than to the real problems of policy issues. If they are not well informed about critical decision points, the research they frame and fund is apt to be wide of the decision mark. In cases in which decisions are made at state or local levels of government, as they are in many social realms from education to corrections, their formulation of research needs is apt to be even less relevant. It appears likely that the less information research formulators have about the policy issue, the less likely are they to frame research that addresses critical questions.

THE ELEMENT OF TIME   Research takes time. A year or two or more elapses from the writing of a research proposal to the presentation of results. Therefore, research formulators have to try to foresee what issues will emerge in the years ahead, rather than simply addressing this year's questions. The difficulties in prediction are legion (Duncan 1969).

Fortunately, few crises burst on the scene with the explosiveness of the "energy crisis" brought on by the rise in oil prices by the Organization of Petroleum Exporting Countries (OPEC) nations. Much of the national agenda is a reprise of earlier years—new attempts to pass national health insurance, modifications in revenue sharing, revisions in federal aid to education. While many of the general issues are familiar, however, it is not always clear which aspect will be the core of controversy and what kind of research information will be required. For issues that involve new programs and a break from tradition, the specification of research presents special difficulties. It therefore seems logical that the newer and more unfamiliar a policy issue, the more difficult it is to foresee the kinds of variables, data, and analytical relationships that will inform the policy debate.

The social sciences operate from a modest knowledge base. There are many low-level empirical generalizations but few empirically based theories of wide generality. Laws of human behavior, equivalent to laws of physical behavior, are notable by their absence (Barton 1974). Therefore, it is difficult to predict or model the behavior of people, groups, and institutions under changed conditions.

Without a firm theoretical basis, social science researchers engage in a great deal of trial-and-error research to meet policy needs. They do special studies to find out which policies and programs work, which components of successful policy are essential and which are tangential to reaching desired outcomes, and which kinds of communities or clienteles are best served by specific programs. There are an almost unlimited number of questions that deserve study, and the task of selection and specification becomes formidable.

RESEARCH METHODS Researchers often choose and conceptualize problems in terms of the methodologies in which they are proficient. They do not pick the research method to suit the problem but almost unwittingly see that aspect of the problem to which their methodology applies. Whether they do laboratory experiments, survey research, or modeling, they tend to formulate questions in terms that their methodology can address.

Some policy issues strain the limits of available research methodologies, posing questions for which methods are inadequate. If policy makers want to know the effects of housing allowances on the supply of housing in a community, for example, there is little previous information on tap and no clear way to find out. The recourse is to carry out an experiment and watch—but an experiment is no mean feat. Small samples will not do; a community has to be as saturated with housing vouchers as it would be in real life. All the poor people eligible must be given vouchers, in order to see whether the cost of renting or buying a house will go up and whether old buildings are improved and new buildings are constructed to fill demand. A long time and a good deal of study would elapse before answers are available; even then, the few communities studied would not be representative of the universe (the nation) in which the program would ultimately be implemented.

Similarly, in some fields, concepts are extremely difficult to measure with existing instruments. For example, few scientists are fully satisfied with the indicators used to measure such complex notions as mental health. Some topics of interest are hard to observe: organizational change is a topic that presses against the limits of methodological know-how. Interviews of people in positions both within and outside the organization may reveal their perceptions of change, but knowledge of real change in the organization's functioning sometimes seems elusive. In this case as in others, there is a need for further development of study methods.

These, then, are some of the cognitive difficulties that affect the formulation of appropriate research. They reflect inadequate knowledge at several levels—by the policy maker and research funder about the specific kinds of knowledge that will clarify policy debate, by the researcher about translation of knowledge needs into concrete research plans, and, most basically, in the theoretical and methodological status of the social sciences. They represent limits on the ability to predict, select, specify, and distill research questions out of the entangled and flowing complexities of the policy world.

Institutional Location

VARYING PERCEPTIONS   Different locations create different perceptions of policy issues. Each set of actors in the policy process responds to the incentives and rewards of their own positions. Legislators may be engaged by the needs of their constituents, the President by the desire for reelection, bureau chiefs by loyalties to the state agencies with which they deal, policy analysts by the desire to achieve a program goal, the staff of the Office of Management and Budget by the desire to cut costs, and researchers by the desire to extend a theoretical formulation. Some may see no need for research at all; others are likely to see divergent questions. The aspect of a problem that is deemed worthy of study varies with each person's view of the problem. The situation suggests that the larger the number of actors who participate in the debate on a policy issue, the more diverse will be both the questions raised and the standards of judgment that will be applied. As a consequence, no single study is likely either to resolve all questions or to be universally accepted as definitive.

Holders of different positions have different perspectives on the kinds of research that are necessary. In talking about cognitive difficulties, we noted that isolation from the policy center can lead to ignorance about issues. Here, we are concerned with the effects of location on perceptions of what the research questions are.

People conceptualize research in ways that fit their view of the core questions in a problem, and their social location affects that view. In particular, it has effects on how quickly "answers" are wanted, and thus, what cut at the problem research can make and which factors in the situation are seen as fixed and which are subject to policy manipulation.

Policy makers tend to be in a hurry. They want action immediately and tend to ignore the long-term aspects of policy issues. They are impatient with research that attempts to explain cause-and-effect relationships, to identify factors that give rise to social problems, or to develop empirically based theories of intervention.[10]

However, every policy represents a causal theory. Every policy says, in effect, that we have set a goal and we will undertake activities A and B because they will achieve that goal. As much recent experience in social programming has indicated, however, policies often fail to reach the goal, and the theories on which they are based become suspect.

In order to develop more adequate policies, we need more adequate theories. To develop better theory, we may need research that addresses basic questions about the factors involved in the origin and persistence of social problems and the kinds of changes that will reverse their effects. To formulate research on this level, social scientists are likely to be more qualified than those closer to immediate events to conceptualize the research questions.

Institutional location also affects which elements in the situation one accepts as given and which are susceptible to change. Policy-related research has to deal with manipulable aspects of the situation. Government officials, partly because of their time perspective, see many aspects of the world as fixed. They accept, for example, the stratification of influence and income as relatively stable conditions. They are likely to focus research attention on variables that can be altered

---

[10] Laurence Lynn, Jr., suggests that all policy makers cannot literally be in a hurry, or no basic research and long-term studies would ever get funded. The "answers now" cast of mind is a tendency, not a fixed mold.

without disrupting basic arrangements. For example, if job training programs are not successful in placing people in jobs, they may call for research on trainees' attitudes and work motivations. They are probably less likely than those further removed from the program to raise questions about job availability, work conditions, opportunities for advancement, and other characteristics of the job market.

The Research Funding Process

If the policy process is complex, so, too, is the research funding process. There is an assortment of mechanisms for obtaining research, which can be classified as (1) procurement, (2) solicitation, and (3) assistance.[11] Each mechanism tends to give a particular set of actors more influence in the formulation of research.

Procurement strategies are modeled on those that are used to buy buttons or weapons systems. Government staff specifies the "product" to be bought and the time allotted and sometimes provides very detailed itemization of the research procedures to be used for developing that product (e.g., questions to be addressed, sample size and location, instruments and measures, analysis procedures, time schedule). Competitive proposals are sought, and the submitted proposals are reviewed, usually by in-house staff, for understanding of the problem, technical merit, cost, and organizational capability. A winning applicant is chosen and a contract is awarded. In the procurement procedure, it is the staff's definitions of research that are dominant.

Solicitation is an invitation to interested researchers to undertake research on any of a list of topics that are of priority interest to an agency. Much more latitude is allowed investigators to choose what they will do and how, but the work is expected to advance the mission of the agency in the specified areas. The review of proposals can be done by staff, often with the assistance of outside consultants. Sometimes panels of outside researchers are convened to approve the scientific merit of proposals while staff considers their relevance to the issues, or outside reviewers can make the final determination of which studies to fund. Multiple awards are made on the same topic. Several researchers can study different aspects of such topics as "fertility behavior of working women" or "dissemination of educational innovations to classroom teachers." Under solicitation procedures, government staff set the frame within which researchers define their studies.

[11] The U.S. Commission of Government Procurement (1972) makes the distinction between procurement and assistance.

Research assistance is support for investigator-initiated research. The agency tends to have lower expectations of immediate and direct contributions of the research to policy decisions. The contributions are expected to be longer-range, perhaps more fundamental, and less dictated by government needs. Contributions to local programs and to professional practice are as welcome as contributions to federal policy. Research proposals tend to be reviewed by panels of peers: the major criterion is research merit, and support usually lasts for several years of study. In research assistance, it is the researchers' formulation of the research that prevails. (See Wirt *et al.* 1974).

In all three procedures, a large number of people are engaged in solicitation, specification, proposal writing, and proposal review. In the lengthy process, some of the impetus for selection of the topic and its component questions may become blunted. As in the children's game of telephone, the message at the beginning may be substantially altered by the time the funded research plan emerges at the end.

The way in which the research is funded affects its formulation. When government staff has tight control, the research is apt to have a shorter time frame and more practical orientation, and it is generally limited to a narrow range of policy options. Bureaucratic pressures on the staff as well as the prevailing view restrict the kind of study that can be done. For example, RFPs have to be cleared with superiors, and the clearance procedure gives a number of people the opportunity to constrict or veto ideas, tending to clamp limits on innovative plans. The researchers who receive contracts through procurement strategies are more apt to be working in commercial research firms than in universities. In such profit-oriented settings, they are likely to accept government staff's research formulations without cavil and change. In such a situation, the bureaucratic view prevails.

With the use of proposal solicitation and especially assistance mechanisms, university-affiliated social scientiests are likely to do the research. Their approach is apt to be more free ranging. Solicitation, more than assistance, aims for a coordinated program of related research, seeking to match research to the topics of the agency's salient concerns. Assistance mechanisms, which rely on the initiative of researchers, often lead to an array of disparate projects. However, research programs funded under all three funding mechanisms have found it difficult to develop a cumulative knowledge base.

BIAS When an agency with a stake in the policy outcome funds research, it may emphasize aspects of the issue most likely to yield results favorable to its own position. Thus, for example, the U.S.

Commission on Civil Rights (1967) supported the research reported as *Racial Isolation in the Public Schools*, which emphasized the cognitive gains of black students in integrated schools. This was by no means the only issue involved in school desegregation, but it was one for which positive evidence was expected. The Civil Rights Commission was a partisan that wanted its policy view to prevail.

Similar biases can occur in evaluations of agency programs. Canny administrators may try to rig the phrasing of the evaluation questions to focus on areas where positive outcomes are clearest. Thus, they may stress numbers of hours of service provided rather than effects of the service on its recipients, or the popularity of programs with children and their parents rather than the gains in achievement or health.[12]

Some funding organizations, even with clear operational missions, maintain the highest standards of integrity and neutrality. Nevertheless, in heavily politicized agencies, I suspect that the more responsibility an agency has for setting policy and maintaining programs, the less autonomy it allows researchers. The stronger its political stake, the more likely is it to formulate research in terms favorable to its position.

STABILITY Another structural difficulty is the piecemeal nature of most social research funding. Research tends to be approved and funded on a project-by-project basis, a procedure that limits continuity in lines of research. Each new project must be proposed and approved separately. Serendipitous findings cannot be followed up, nor promising leads pursued.

Other options exist. If legislative mandate allows, an agency can create and fund an outside research organization to do its work, as the Air Force did with the Rand Corporation after World War II or the Department of Housing and Urban Development did with the Urban Institute in 1968. In this kind of arrangement, the agency can provide unrestricted funds for a core staff with additional funding through regular grant and contract channels. Alternatively, an agency can fund a research organization to carry on a "program" of research: the research organization submits an application, usually in competition with other applicants, for long-term support of five years or more. The application specifies the objectives and nature of the research to be conducted and the qualifications of the staff, but, once approved, programmatic support usually allows the investigators considerable latitude.

---

[12] McDill *et al.* (1969) note that the popularity model of evaluation is a sure winner in educational programs.

Most important for our discussion, there is a lack of stability in the research personnel funded to do the work. Researchers come and go, and few build up the body of experience that would enable them to develop deep understanding of policy issues over time. Each new crop has to learn the arena, the issues, the political constraints, and the range of acceptable options. This, too, has an effect on the formulation of research. To the extent that researchers frame the study, the effect is direct; to the extent that they respond to agency formulations, the effect is less direct but may permeate the development of the study in more subtle ways.

INTERPRETING RESEARCH FINDINGS

Communication Style

One of the cognitive problems in getting research findings into the policy sphere is that most communication is written, and the writing of research reports tends to be turgid. Researchers are prone to what others call jargon (although for the social scientist, the jargon may be a precise shorthand for complex concepts). Some terms are unfamiliar to policy makers, and they receive few interpretive clues. More serious, the concepts that the terms embody are not well understood. The whole conceptual apparatus that has supported the research is sometimes misconstrued.

The solution, then, is not only to write shorter reports or more lucid prose but also to find ways to bridge the conceptual differences that underlie complaints about bad writing. The theoretical orientations embedded in a study cannot and should not be excised or smoothed over—they should be made explicit. If the assumptions are unpalatable to decision makers, the disagreement should be clarified and faced. For example, a sociological study may take for granted that one's social affiliations—class, ethnicity, occupational position, and religious affiliation—have a strong influence on behavior. To a policy maker with an individualized view of the world, in which all control their own destinies, the premises are philosophically unacceptable and the findings would be dismissed. However, the policy maker should have to confront the divergence in premises and recognize the basis on which he is dismissing the study.

Some policy makers reject the whole notion of quantitative research and statistical generalizations about people. In a current study on the usability of social research, we have found a number of psychiatrists and other clinicians in this category. They believe in the uniqueness of the individual and their own perceptions and judgment, so abstract and probabilistic generalizations cut no ice with them. Whatever its beauty or brevity, they are unlikely to put much trust in a social research report—much less find it useful.

Sophisticated statistics may impede, rather than aid, the policy maker's comprehension of research. Whereas they are a boon to the researcher, providing greater explanatory power, to the policy maker they are a block to intuitive understanding. Once nonprofessionals could look at means, percentage differences, or correlation coefficients and do some interpretation (and checking of the author's interpretation) on their own. Now, with regression analysis and more complex multivariate analyses, they are at the mercy of the researchers' interpretation and have to put greater trust in researchers' competence and objectivity.[13] In some cases, this demands more trust than they are willing to give.

The Nature of Research Findings

Some research findings provide no clear-cut conclusions. The data relationships are small and inconsistent, and the variables studied account for a small fraction of the variance. No clear highway to recommendations, no course of action, no obvious remedy opens up. To move from this kind of shapeless research to action is a heavy intellectual burden.

Moreover, in many areas the studies are not cumulative. They do not add to a gradually increasing fund of tested knowledge. Rather, results are inconsistent over a series of studies that seem to have been done in parallel situations. As new research is initiated to clarify the factors that account for divergent outcomes, it tends to branch and fork, occasionally creating not less confusion but more. Unknown and unmeasured variables with strong effects apparently abound, and the search for them leads in several directions, with different investigators taking different paths. Knowledge, instead of cumulating, in some cases appears to fragment.

One example of this lack of cumulativeness comes from evaluation of Head Start programs. An early and partial review of evaluation results from the years 1965–67 (McDill et al. 1969, pp. 19, 66) showed that "eleven of the thirty-one studies appear to have shown clearly positive effects of Head Start experiences on cognitive development. . . . [W]e should attempt to answer the question of which of the

[13] I wish to thank Janet Weiss for bringing this situation to my attention.

alternative methods appear most successful. . . ." Head Start Planned Variations was a noble attempt to do just that: to implement a set of curriculum models, developed and sponsored by educators to evaluate their relative effectiveness. By 1975, extensive evaluation data (Cohen 1975, p. 150) indicated that:

None of the models consistently did better than their comparisons—good results in one year did not repeat in the next. Secondly, in no cases did *all* experimental sites in a model clearly perform at higher levels than their comparisons. And third, no consistent pattern of differences in effectiveness emerged among the sponsored treatments. The evaluations show a few cases in which particular sponsors produced greater gains than others. But these gains were inconsistent across the tests used in the experiment.

To determine whether the curricular models affected different children in different ways, further analysis (Smith 1975, p. 110) was done:

Though the models that showed substantial effects [on any of the test batteries used] were not equally successful for all types of children, there were no major disordinal interactions between model and child—that is, no model that was effective on the average for a certain test was particularly effective for one type of child and particularly ineffective for another.

One of the major effects of 10 years of study on Head Start was to reopen long-settled questions about the adequacy of tests, exactly what IQ and achievement tests were measuring, and whether the scores meant much about success.

Because research is unpredictable and no one can be sure what information will emerge, there are times when the findings are overly familiar. They support what people already know intuitively, by experience, or through earlier research. Decision makers tend to look at research of this kind with a so-what-else-is-new cynicism. Of course, there is value in reinforcing popular wisdom and replicating previous findings: knowledge builds and confidence in it grows, but some policy makers see little intellectual or policy payoff in repeating what they feel is obvious.

The Context of Research Application

A critical element in the interpretation of research for action derives from the concrete circumstances of the situation in which results will be applied. Research typically deals with predictions that, as Merton says (1949), conveniently assume that the large number of other factors remains constant. But when research results are destined for application at an actual time and place, it is foolish to assume that other factors will remain constant. The researcher has to estimate which factors in the concrete situation will change and how. Merton elaborates this idea (p. 175):

(a) Every applied research must include some speculative inquiry into the role of diverse factors which can only be roughly assessed, not meticulously studied.

(b) The validity of the concrete forecast depends upon the degree of (non-compensated) error in *any* phase of the total inquiry. The weakest links in the chain of applied research may typically consist of the *estimates* of contingent conditions under which the investigated variables will *in fact* operate.

(c) To this degree, the recommendations for policy do not flow directly and exclusively from the *research*. Recommendations are the product of the research *and* the estimates of contingent conditions, these estimates not being of the same order of probability or precision as the more abstract interrelations examined in the research itself.

(d) Such contingencies make for indeterminacy of the recommendations derived from the research and thus create a gap between research and policy.

Just as research has to move from the abstract to the concrete, it has to move from the past (when the research was done) to the future (when it will be applied). The researcher has to assess future trends and their probable impact on observed relationships. Thus, for example, the early evaluations of methadone treatment for heroin users were based on carefully selected subjects in the few existing treatment facilities. Results looked good—but what would happen when eligibility standards were removed and scores of treatment centers were opened to everyone who applied? The effects, it turns out, were less dramatic, and some counterproductive side effects appeared: a drug culture of persons maintained on methadone appeared; their commitment to school or work was no greater than it had been with heroin. Could the early researchers have estimated the effects of large-scale methadone programs? If they had, would those estimates have affected the policies adopted?

APPLYING RESEARCH TO POLICY ISSUES

Besides affecting research formulation, social structural factors account for much of the gap between research and policy. Researchers and policy makers tend to have disparate understandings, norms, and values. Their differences derive partly from the processes of self-selection and institutional recruitment into different careers, and partly from the influence of the institutions in which they work.

Different Perspectives

Researchers have to make choices about which data to highlight, which relationship among variables to emphasize, and how much attention and what kind of interpretation to give to the vast array of "facts." For example, is it "only" 21 percent who took jobs, or "fully" 21 percent who took jobs? What surprises them? What framework do they choose for making sense out of the piles of computer output? Lynn (1973, p. 57) observes:

The choices of conceptual frameworks, assumptions, output measures, variables, hypotheses, and data provide wide latitude for judgment, and values of the researcher often guide decisions to at least some degree.

As important as this is in the early phases of research, it is perhaps even more profound at the end. In moving from analysis of data to recommendations for action, researchers must leave the world of fact and science. Rarely are the data clear-cut and authoritative enough to indicate the path to a predetermined goal. Usually, researchers must make a conscious leap into the realm of "ought"; guidance for the leap comes partly from the data but partly from their own values. Policy researchers are likewise constrained by their interpretation of the policy feasibilities—what is possible given current arrangements and resources.

I noted earlier that social scientists tend to be a particularly liberal group. The values that they espouse tend to lead them to favor the poor, victims of discrimination or bureaucratic inertia, and clients of service agencies rather than the agencies giving service.

Coleman (1974) did an interesting "rough" analysis of 38 research studies sponsored by a variety of commercial firms, government departments, and service agencies (Figure 6). He looked at whether the

Recommendations Derived from Point of View of	Researcher's Position	
	Producer's Agent	Agent of Third Party or Independent
Producer Interests	11	2
Consumer Interests	12	13

FIGURE 6   Coleman's analysis of 38 research studies.

researchers developed recommendations from the point of view of th
agency (what he calls the "producer of goods or services") or from th
point of view of the clients (the consumers of goods or services). H
does not suggest that producer and consumer interests were necessar
ily opposed, but, ordinarily, they coincided only in part. He als
looked at the relationship of the research to the producer: whether th
research was supported by the agency or whether it was funded by
third party (such as a foundation) or independently. The data show tha
in general researchers tend to look at things through consumers' eyes
by a ratio of about 2:1. When a third party funds the research
researchers favor consumers by more than 6:1. Even when the pro
ducer foots the bill, the ratio drops to only 1:1. In other words, at leas
half of the research paid for by an operating agency derives it
perspective from the interests of the consumers rather than the man
agers. When the researchers are financially independent of the produc
ers, they give almost exclusive attention to consumer interests.

From government officials concerned with policy, on the other hand
we can probably expect the producer's interpretation. They are con
cerned with feasibility: implementation, costs, and smooth operation
When research is not only supported by government but also initiated
monitored, and closely supervised by government staff, the tenor and
tone are apt to derive from the interests of those in charge.

While a study is in progress, the issues with which it deals often
change. Matters that were once thought central are resolved or become
irrelevant; new problems take center stage. Thus, for example, Cohen
(1975) found that, during the course of the evaluation of the Follow
Through Planned Variations, the original priority of pupils' gains in
achievement on standardized tests lost its salience. For one thing, the
appropriateness of the tests as a measure of achievement became
doubtful. More basically, questions arose about the usefulness of
school achievement itself as a predictor of later social and economic
success. Moreover, the opinions of activist groups in education swung
away from concern about school curriculum (regarded earlier as a
source of school success or failure) and toward issues of decentraliza
tion of educational administration and community control. By the time
the data were available, they were largely irrelevant to the contemporary policy debate (Cohen 1975): "The longer the experiments continued the more doubts were raised about their premises, and the more
it seemed that other issues, discovered along the way, were more
fundamental."

Similar obsolescence of issues, at an even faster pace, was revealed
in review of a study on the federal student loan program (Weiss 1970).
Over the one-year period that the study was in progress, questions

about consolidation of loan programs had been resolved and new questions about loans held by student demonstrators were engaging the Congress.

The policy debate rarely waits for research reports. Ironically, research that is tied too closely to the immediate issues, that proceeds from exclusively practical assumptions with little potential for generalization, runs the risk of falling behind the pace of policy making.

Dissemination

The lack of channels for regularized dissemination of research results is a major cause of their neglect. Often, few of the persons involved in decisions learn of research that could reduce the degree of uncertainty. Even when research is expressly commissioned by government agencies, it sometimes fails to reach the appropriate "user." Research done at a farther remove, under a grant or through nongovernmental support, has a more circuitous and stony path to the proper audience.

There are even worse things in the realm of dissemination: government-funded projects that never submit a report, investigators who regard a research grant as a personal benefice rather than a commitment to produce knowledge, projects that drift off the agreed-upon topic and report on subjects unforeseen and unwanted by government sponsors, who try to cover up research reports that reveal their agencies or programs in an unfavorable light.

Computerized information retrieval systems seem to be of little use to decision makers (Caplan *et al.*, 1975, pp. 13–14). They are too unselective, perhaps too forbidding with their complicated hardware, and usually seem to produce too many reams of undigested printout. People are more dynamic conveyors of information, but government agencies have few staff whose jobs are to move information to the points at which it is needed.

Dissemination tends to be nobody's job. Neither government research managers, project officers, nor researchers win kudos by matching research results with policy needs. Each group gets its rewards in its own bailiwick—from colleagues and fellow professionals or from those who control career chances. Nobody has a stake in "audience satisfaction," so the dissemination office is practically empty.

Diffusion

Almost all discussions of the use of research in policy making start from the premise that at some discernible place and time, policy actually gets "made," that there are people who singly and collectively make specific arrangements to solve a problem. The assumption that there are actors who make a policy sometimes contradicts reality.

In some circumstances, it is difficult to locate any people who are charged with the responsibility for making a decision. Alkin *et al.* (1974, p. 94) writes about educational programs:

> Identification of the project's decision maker(s) is perhaps the most elusive aspect of organizing an evaluation effort. Different organizations characteristically have very different decision structures ranging from those in which specific decision responsibility is emphasized to those in which rather amorphous divisions of decision-making responsibility exist. The spectrum of potential decision makers is equally diffuse. . . .

Amorphous and diffuse decision structures rarely produce clear-cut decisions. Rather, options somehow are progressively narrowed by a series of almost imperceptible choices. A variegated and uncoordinated group of people takes minor steps. The pattern of organizational behavior slowly moves along the same or a somewhat changed direction. Without conscious effort, a defined locus of decision, or people charged with responsibility for decision, a decision accretes.

Even in legislatures, in which voting seems to be the ideal type of decisional activity, the vote often serves only to ratify decisions made beforehand. The choices were made in legislative committee or the executive agency that drafted the bill or even earlier—in interest groups, professional groups, or staff conclaves. Some of those choices, too, are not conscious selections among alternative courses, but the effect of drift: there is a progressive constriction of options as consensus gradually grows that one course of action is appropriate.

In these kinds of diffuse and subtle processes, the purposeful use of social research is inconceivable. The only kind of use possible is the almost imperceptible absorption of concepts and knowledge from an array of sources, unreferenced and uncatalogued, but slowly changing the climate of opinion.

Even when authority for decisions is clearly lodged in specific positions, those who hold those positions may stay on the job only for short periods. Turnover in personnel can limit attention to research in two ways. First, it may encourage decision makers to consider short-term activity rather than long-term effects. Knowing that they will stay for only a short time, they may be interested simply in doing something, no matter how well- or ill-conceived, to satisfy constituents. They concentrate their attention on takeoffs rather than landings, since they may not be around to reap the fruits of their decisions. Second, because of changes in the top personnel of government agencies, continuity of attention to issues may suffer. If a new man or woman comes in, he or she may have little interest in the particular issue, or the facet of the issue, on which research was commissioned. When the study results are reported, the new incumbent may not be interested. Since the questions are not his or her questions, the answers may seem irrelevant.

Political appointees in federal departments, at the level of assistant secretary and above, usually stay in their jobs for about two years; about half stay less than two years (Stanley *et al*. 1967). Among civil servants, there is less turnover but there is movement from one position to another. As most researchers know from experience, research project officers in government agencies shift jobs or assignments at what seems a whirlwind rate. The project officer with whom one deals about the substance and mechanics of a research grant or contract may change two or three times in the course of a study.

Turnover is not necessarily bad. New policy makers may bring a greater zest for knowledge, a zeal to bone up and master the field. Their enthusiasm can spark heightened attention to research.[14] The possibility exists, however, that people leaving a position may take their files, their knowledge, and their curiosity with them, thereby erasing the departmental memory. One could reasonably surmise that the greater the turnover in policy positions, the less likely is commissioned research to have an impact on decisions.

Fragmentation of Authority

Sometimes, the government agency concerned with a problem (and the research) does not have the authority to make a decision implied by the research conclusions. The decision may lie in the bailiwick of another agency, for example, research suggesting that children's educational achievement will be improved by better health care or that delinquency will be reduced by more relevant school curricula. To implement such recommendations would require massive efforts at coordination across departments, fields of specialization, and responsibility. In some cases, there is no department or public body that is empowered to make decisions of the scope suggested.

An example of this kind of problem is reported by Rose (1974, pp. 135–37) in an interview study of the usefulness of housing statistics to public officials in Scotland. He concluded:

There is no central decision-making mechanism for housing policy. Powers are divided between central and local government, within local government and

---

[14] Caplan's study (Caplan *et al*. 1975) found that federal officials who did not plan to stay in government were more likely to use social science information.

between public and private sectors. It follows from the above that there is no client for an integrated information system that monitors housing supply and demand, because there is no public agency which has terms of reference and objectives as broad as those encompassed by theorists of public choice and social indicators. . . . The alternative to the above conclusions is easily stated but difficult to secure. It is to change the structure of government to create a central point for the review of housing policy. As and when this might happen, an information system could be provided to assist such a body in exercising public choice. If this were to occur in the field of housing, it would be a major innovation. It would achieve a degree of centralization of policy-making that even the Prime Minister himself has yet to achieve in what is nominally but not always accurately described as central government.

The problem of fragmented policy decision making is even more prevalent in the federal system of the United States with its complex amalgamation of overlapping jurisdictions. If radical centralization of governmental powers would be necessary to permit more rational use of knowledge, the remedy is probably far less acceptable than the problem.

The lack of fit between the authority of public bodies and the scope of research implications can limit application even of seemingly simple recommendations. Within a single agency, an operational change may require approval from different bureaus on budget, personnel, job duties, agency relationships, physical facilities, etc. Not every party to the decision will be impressed by the same type of research evidence. At the other extreme, it can be argued that there are few changes of even monumental range that cannot be implemented through action of the President and the Congress. But at those altitudes, potential users are integrating scores of inputs and no research study or body of research can be expected to have more than peripheral influence (Dreyfus 1976).

The Political Environment

Whatever research shows, the political climate places limits on what kinds of change will be countenanced, how fast, and at what cost. Not only partisan politics and administration politics but also agency politics help to determine the range of acceptable options. In the broadest sense, the opinion of the public indicates what is acceptable and what is not. Thus, for example, Jencks' call for socialism to increase equality, since his study (Jencks *et al*. 1972) indicates that education does not do the job, is unlikely to be heeded; neither government nor public is ready to contemplate such a step.

It would seem that the further removed research conclusions and recommendations are from mainstream opinion or the opinion of major groups, the less likely are the results to influence policy in the short run.

This limitation of the social structure on the implementation of research—that is, the constraint of political context—is not only a constraint but is also an important corrective. Researchers are not all-wise. Their creative minds and imaginations may lead to research pregnant with potential for fundamental social change, and their recommendations may occasionally urge basic reforms in the institutions of society. But a democratic society, through its duly constituted representatives, has a say about its destiny. It has no more obligation to accept the data and dicta of social scientists than it does to listen to shamans, astrologers, or television commentators. Nor should the value interpretations of the researcher be smuggled into the policy debate under the guise of "scientific evidence." Judgments have to be acknowledged for what they are and take their place alongside the judgments of other policy actors. Social scientists serve not as final arbiters but as information purveyors, analysts, evaluators, critics, goads, and interpreters to legitimate political representatives.

Policy makers for their part are interested not only in the application of research evidence to public decisions but also in representing interests and values, reconciling differences, and reaching compromises that maintain the stability of the system. Theirs is political rationality rather than scientific rationality. They may neglect research in their service of other functions, but, from their point of view, the use of research is not necessarily the highest good.

Limited Resources

Some research suggests exciting new directions for policy, but at times of recession or when other actitivies drain the federal budget, there may be insufficient resources to invest in new policy initiatives. Nor are financial resources the only constraint. On occasion, there may be shortages of facilities, qualified staff, or motivated managers. In an interesting attempt to promote the use of research, Glaser and Ross (1971) disseminated evaluation results of a successful weekend therapy program.[15] Despite interest, few agencies implemented the program; they ran afoul not only of ideological resistances but also of such practical problems as agencies' lack of overnight living quarters for

---

[15]Their report deals with an attempt at Type 4 utilization, i.e., the adoption of an innovative program "certified" by evaluation research.

participants and staff's dislike of working on weekends. It seems likely that the greater the resources required to apply research results, the less likely is research alone to convince decision makers of the appropriate course.

Conclusion

In sum, problems in the application of research results derive in large part from characteristics of the political sphere into which they move. Much of what happens in the bureaus, departments, and legislative halls is beyond the control of researchers. If they have done a relevant and competent study, if it reaches people who can use it, and if it is intelligible to them, then they have done their job. Extensive personal contact and briefings can increase the likelihood that the study is noticed and that it doesn't get cut off at the pass by lower-echelon officials who seek to keep it from their superiors,[16] but even such activities cannot guarantee that it will be heeded. When research is alien to decision makers' sense of the situation, their political beliefs, or their interests, the most intensive dissemination of its results will not have much effect.

Some observers (see Rule 1971) believe that all social problems are basically political issues and that "conditions like pollution, racism, and the like are basically oppositions of interest—not social problems but social conflicts, overt or concealed." In this view, research and expertise must take sides in the conflict; if researchers work to solve problems as a government agency defines them, then they are supporting the interests and purposes of those in power (p. 48):

For there can be no definition of a "social problem" which does not involve political judgments, nor certainly any "solution" to such problems devoid of partisan content. And to pretend otherwise merely leads to the introduction of partisan measures and objectives in the guise of nonpolitical technocratic "problem solving."

It is not necessary to accept so sweeping a characterization in order to recognize the point. There are issues and problems on which an overwhelming majority of Americans agree on both the nature of the problem and the zone of solution. However, the formulation and the application of research involve judgments, and the judgments of actors in the policy research process diverge.

[16] The story of Wohlstetter's activities in bringing the Rand Corporation's Strategic Bases Study to the attention of military decision makers is a classic case of extensive and canny lobbying for research results and recommendations (Smith 1966).

LEVERS OF CHANGE

What features of the research-to-policy process can be altered? The factors most immediately amenable to change are procedures both for the definition and funding of research and for dissemination of results. The proposed solutions in these domains tend to be offered by social scientists in government or sometimes by social science consultants to government—people who have a stake in improving the working of the system and know the procedural ropes. The character of the proffered solutions bears the imprint of their interests. (This discussion is abbreviated, because the National Research Council's Study Panel on Social Research and Development has given extensive consideration to these factors. The purpose of this paper is to analyze the relationship of proposed remedies to the obstacles just described.)

Forecasting Research Needs

Better prediction of knowledge needs hinges on better prediction of policy issues. More thought should go into looking ahead so that newly funded research is not concentrating on last year's problems but addressing those that loom ahead. All too often, research follows rather than precedes public recognition of a problem. Only when the problem has been recognized and funds appropriated is money available for research. By that time, the problems are upon us and there are demands for immediate action. Little lead time remains for research.

But I have become less exercised over the problem of timing than I used to be. It is unequivocal that research reported after the issue it deals with has been resolved is not as useful as it would have been earlier, but most domestic issues are not resolved once and for all. Except for initiation of a major new activity, such as federal entry into the funding of education, issues tend to be dealt with on a piecemeal basis: programs are developed, resources are allocated, structures and procedures are set up for implementation. In the course of administering the policy, revisions are made in all phases on a continuing basis: the level of appropriations changes, programs are revised, structures are modified. Therefore, research knowledge continues to be relevant to the policy.

Research can contribute to reconsideration of (1) the basic goals of a policy ("Should the federal government assume responsiblity for improving the mental health of the populace?"); (2) the means through which goals are to be achived ("Should the federal government encourage and support community mental health centers?"); (3) the amount of public funding allocated to the activity ("How much should the government pay toward the establishment and support of centers?"); and (4) its ongoing administration ("What activities of treatment, prevention, and education should be conducted and how can they best be carried out?"). Research is relevant not only to the original making of policy but also to the inevitable remakings of policy and even (maybe especially) to the unmaking of policy. When a policy has been ineffective and officals seek to terminate it, research can be a particularly useful source of information about its failings and likely alternatives.

It is true, though, that over time the shape of the policy discussion changes. The topics on which research evidence is sought in later years are not necessarily the topics that were fashionable at the time a program of research was begun. Thus, an overly narrow research focus may turn out to be counterproductive. More wide-ranging work that can be generalized beyond the immediacies of the present situation may retain its relevance long beyond the use-life of specific-problem-oriented studies.

Planning a Program of Research

Social science research programs in mission agencies need planning. As a framework for planning, they need a sense of research needs as policy makers define them. As noted earlier, however, policy makers are frequently unable to formulate their research needs adequately. The solution thus cannot be a quick survey or even a sophisticated survey of "what data will make a difference in decisions." These kinds of questions are too difficult for off-the-cuff answers. Moreover, different members of the policy-making process will nominate different issues and subtopics.

Probably only continuous contact with decision makers and involvement in policy questions will help planners to choose appropriate areas for research emphasis. Such contacts should not be limited to one set of officials. Varied constituencies, organized and unorganized, can be consulted for their views of policy problematics. Diversity of perspective seems a prerequisite for planning an effective research program. Research results will emerge over a span of years and have to satisfy knowledge needs of many actors, present and future.

Planning procedures can be tinkered with and probably rationalized. But rationality of process is not always accompanied by rationality of product. Planning can introduce its own irrelevancies. Systematic planning can probably direct attention to some areas that have been overlooked and others that have been overworked. Some wholesome effects are likely to ensue, but procedural remedies cannot solve basic problems. If no consensus exists on priorities among issues or the amenability of stubborn problems to research, planning systems cannot impose them.

Supporting Research

Government officials seeking to tailor research programs to perceived policy needs often look at funding mechanisms as a lever of control. The basic dilemma is that the mechanisms that increase researchers' responsiveness to agency-defined needs also seem to decrease research quality. RFPs give the government agency the greatest control, institutional or programmatic support the least, and there has been a widespread belief that the short-order contract research procured by RFP has less technical competence than research done by institutions with long-range support.[17]

Why does the funding mechanism seem to make a difference? Why does there seem to be an association between long-term research support and research quality? The reasons are many: the kinds of research groups that receive institutional or programmatic support are usually chosen specifically because of their expertise and competence; ongoing support can (although it does not always) provide continuity of attention and research and a long-term familiarity with the issue arena; government places fewer time restrictions and methodological imperatives on institutionally supported researchers, so they are not subjected to the constraints that contract researchers face; the kinds of problems that are addressed are different. Researchers with long-term support can select issues, or topics within issues, that are most suitably investigated given current knowledge and available research methodologies. They can also select issues that hold the greatest promise for generalizable and theoretically relevant findings, so that they have high motivation to do capable research.

Merely changing the funding mechanism will not alter the surrounding conditions. The attempt to reap the benefits purportedly associated with institutional support has led to a series of institutional innovations of highly variable success: HUD's establishment of the Urban Institute; the Office of Economic Opportunity and the Wisconsin Institute for

---

[17] Biderman and Sharp conducted a study of the RFP-funded evaluation research "industry." Their reports (1972, 1974) give a great deal of the flavor of the unstable research world of competitive bidding.

Poverty Research; the Office of Education and the R&D Centers, educational labs, and educational policy centers; the Social and Rehabilitation Service and its regional research institutes. The range in both quality of work and relevance to policy is mammoth. Long-term support alone, without the surrounding conditions, does not guarantee excellence of research.

Can the choice of the proper mechanism ensure that researchers address questions of high policy priority? Certainly the RFP is well suited to obtaining the kind of research that government officials ask for. The whole procedure—government statement, competitive proposals, staff review—works to encourage responsiveness to government definition of the research problem. However, its value depends on officials' knowing what knowledge is needed. If their formulation of the research problem is inadequate, then there are few correctives in the system; the research organizations that specialize in contract research are unlikely to criticize: theirs is not to reformulate but to do what is asked. The knowledge "products" that emerge from contract research tend to be so specific that they have little transferability

Agencies have made an effort to secure both responsiveness to immediate research needs and the long-term continuity of relationship associated with "program support" through a relatively new mechanism—the basic ordering agreement. The procedure begins with a competitive request for qualifications and involves a two-tier selection. First, research organizations submit a statement of their qualifications for a particular field of inquiry; after review, a limited number are chosen. They are the only organizations that receive the agency's requests for needed research; competition is limited to the inside few. Thus, they maintain a continuing relationship with the agency, understand its problems and the constraints on its actions, and put this awareness to work in the series of studies they undertake on call. Responsiveness to government need remains high, and to it is added familiarity with subject matter and policy domain.

However, there have been difficulties in this procedure, too. Legal problems have occasionally arisen about long-term exclusion of competitors. Furthermore, the agency is limited to the talents of the "house" organizations. When it comes to replying to the agency's research requests, few research organizations maintain a large idle staff who can be assigned to the new task. Qualified staff are engaged or other studies, and, if the organization wishes to respond to the research request, it has to hire new people—thus undoing the vaunted advantages of continuity. If it does not hire additional personnel, it cannot responsibly do the research. Clearly, the search for the ideal funding mechanism does not end with this arrangement.

Each funding mechanism sets up a chain of events that implicates further choices. For example, the mechanism selected tends to determine the kind of research organization that will respond and do the work.[18] It is difficult to select out the advantages of a mechanism without trundling behind the constellation of disadvantages and irrelevancies that go along with it.

Perhaps more central than the funding procedure is the extent of staff control. There is something about staff control that leads to one kind of research and something about open application that leads to another. When it works well, staff control optimizes short-run relevance. When open application works well, it optimizes longer-run contributions to knowledge.

Choosing Appropriate Research Institutions and Investigators

One of the reasons for altering funding mechanisms and research solicitation procedures is to change the type of research organization and the type of researcher who does the work. Experience has suggested to some observers that academics do high quality research but are unresponsive to the problems formulated by government. Moreover, it is said that they are chronically late in completing their research and are prone to "academization" of their reports. Conversely, commercial research firms are often viewed as willing to accommodate research requests formulated by government staff, prompt in completion, and staffed by writers of a comprehensible if undistinguished prose; on the other hand, they are seen as less skilled in advanced research techniques and prone to corner cutting (even of uncuttable corners) in their zeal to meet contract requests and deadlines.

Such blanket generalizations go well beyond the data. Interviews with some 25 research managers in HEW in 1973 (Consad Research Corporation 1973) indicated that in their experience there was far less predictability. Academic, nonprofit, and for-profit research organizations were not uniform categories. Academic research groups varied as much from one another as they did from the nonprofit or for-profit groups, and the same was true for each of the types. Moreover, their

---

[18] Universities have difficulty responding to RFPs (see McCrone and Hoppin 1973). In some research programs, for-profit organizations are ineligible for grants.

strong conviction was that researchers within a research organization varied, too, and they could not predict the performance of a research team within an organization, even on the basis of previous experience with the same organization.

It seems clear that there is great variability in research performance. The researcher's location—in an academic department, a university research center, a nonprofit institute, or a for-profit firm—accounts for only part of the variation. Location has strong effects, but these categories are not ideal descriptors. Knowing only that certain investigators work in a university is to know something about the kinds of research they are likely to undertake but not much about their competence or policy orientation. Choosing the one "right" researcher is usually beyond the capacity of the funder's knowledge, the viability of the research application as a device to predict excellence, or legal restrictions against favoritism.

Reviewing Research Applications

Another element that can be readily altered is the review procedure. The usual recommendation for change (often hotly debated) is to take review out of the exclusive jurisdiction of peer review panels, who are experts on research merit but uninterested or unqualified to consider relevance to decisions. At the moment, a limited consensus seems to have emerged: peer review panels are as good a device as any for screening proposals for technical merit, and nobody wants to base decisions on invalid research.

To highlight the policy relevance of proposed research, a two-stage review may be useful. Proposals would be reviewed by research peers for technical merit, and federal staff, with the aid of "policy-issue" experts, would review them for their policy utility. Procedures for selecting "policy-issue" reviewers would need thoughtful consideration.

Monitoring Research Performance

Government staff tend to put a great deal of emphasis on monitoring research performance. Their experience suggests that close contact with research in progress tends to keep it honest, on time, and technically competent. It also smoothes the way through the booby traps of forms clearance, requirements for the use of government computers, and other such time-taking snares. The conduct, rather than the formulation or application of research, is what is monitored, but monitoring has consequences at other stages of the research-to-policy process.

Reviewing Completed Research

The NSF-RANN program is instituting a scheme to send final reports routinely to experts for technical review. In those cases in which NSF pays for reproduction of a report, it plans to require that these reviews be incorporated as an appendix. This serves two functions. First, it gives the reader a sense of the strengths and limitations of the research, which findings have a solid and which a not-so-solid foundation, and how firmly the recommendations derive from the empirical findings. Thus, readers (and potential users) are alerted to the sections of the report that they should take most seriously on the basis of internal and external validity. Second, it limits smoke-screen claims of "poor research quality" as an excuse for policy makers' ignoring good research if they dislike the message.

Improving Dissemination

The first way to improve dissemination is for researchers to write better. The classic injunctions are: start a report with a brief summary of the results, avoid jargon, write graceful prose, use charts, maps, and other attractive graphics, interpret the meaning of statistical statements, and write in terms that have meaning to the policy audience.[19]

Another device to improve communication is to set up systematic procedures for getting research to users. Involving potential users in the conduct of the study, for example, has mutual benefits: it makes the study more relevant to their views and establishes their interest in and commitment to its use. If potential users can be involved as advisers on the conclusions and recommendations of the study, so much the better. At the federal level, however, time is such a rare commodity that only in exceptional cases will high-level policy makers consent to serve in such roles, and then usually only if they are already committed to the study of a particular issue.

Various arrangements have been tried to institutionalize interaction. In 1972–1973, HEW set up a system of policy implication papers (PIPS). Research managers were asked to write statements of the implications for policy of the studies funded by their programs. The statements were sent to program chiefs in the department for whom the implications

---

[19] For some of these ideas and others, see the review by Knezo (1974).

were relevant. Thus, research managers in the National Institute for Mental Health were to review their studies not only for implications for community mental health centers but also for such programs as Upward Bound or Medicare and send PIPs to the operators of those programs. The program staffs were to reply, indicating whether they had changed policy, and if not, why not.

PIPs flopped. Not only was the work load severe, but also the research managers did not know what programs were run in the enormous department, who ran them, what their policies were, or what research might relate to them. Further, they were acutely uncomfortable trying to generalize policy recommendations for other people's programs on the basis of one or two studies.

Other inventions have tried to bridge the gap. The office of the Assistant Secretary for Planning and Evaluation in HEW for some years funded an abstracting service to summarize results of research for which it had contracted. Several large volumes of abstracts were prepared, and were occasionally used. (The service was discontinued in 1974.) In 1974–1975, the RANN program of NSF funded critical syntheses of existing research in fields of municipal systems and human resources. The aim was to collect available research and assess its scientific merit, evaluate its utility for decisions, and aggregate the knowledge into a set of propositions or guides to action[20] for the use of officials facing decisions. Although it is too early for feedback, the approach looks promising—more promising than attempts to report the results of one study at a time. Decision makers usually want to know—or should want to know—how the latest set of findings fits into what is already known. It remains to be seen who makes use of the research synthesis, how, and how often.

Another suggestion, oft-touted and rarely instituted, is to set up a dissemination or broker staff, whose mission would be to disseminate research not to the public but to the policy maker. There is very little likelihood that such a maverick office would take root, since it serves neither policy makers' nor researchers' purposes and would not have the ear of anybody of importance. Only by integrating research dissemination directly into the planning and programming system does it stand a chance of claiming attention.

Probably the best organizational channel for research dissemination is the internal planning and analysis office. Staff in these offices are responsible for developing policy options and analyzing the pros and cons of existing and projected policies. In their work, they need the

[20] Harvey Averch, personal communication, June 1975.

best available information, so they seek out existing knowledge and examine its merits and limitations. As they incorporate research into their position papers, they provide policy makers with research results in digested form, cut to fit the issues they face (Weiss 1974). Of course, there are opportunities in the process for distortion, but analytic staffs have the advantages of being in place and having the ear of policy makers. They play an important role in the development of policy, and they have an interest in good information. If there are to be intermediaries between research and policy, analytic staffs appear to have high potential for filling the role.

Extra agency channels are another means of dissemination, since newspapers and general magazines are a major source of reference for policy makers (Weiss 1974). Gone are the days when only the sensational study was judged newsworthy; now thoughtful attention is paid to many kinds of studies. Research associated with newsworthy sources, such as that done for national commissions or reported at congressional hearings, is particularly likely to find its way into print. With greater help from the social science communities in focusing attention and interpreting their work, journalists and commentators can become important linkage agents.[21]

An article in the *New York Times Magazine*, *Psychology Today*, *Newsweek*, or *Harpers* has several advantages. It reaches officials not only of one department but of many departments, the White House staff, and the Congress. The public knows about it, too, so that it counteracts the centralized monopoly on knowledge that federal research sponsorship tends to promote. People in different spheres interact around the same knowledge base. There is a better chance of research being reported in full and in context, rather than having snippets selected to buttress a case while other evidence remains buried. Clearly there are limits on what the media can and will do in research dissemination, and the potential for bias and misuse exists; nevertheless, they remain a noteworthy resource.

Matching Solutions to Problems

The most interesting aspect of this brief look at proposed solutions is their correspondence (or lack of it) to the problems discussed in the preceding section. The solutions that are in vogue are largely administrative remedies, but cognitive problems require cognitive remedies,

---

[21] Thomas F. Pettigrew (1973) suggests that social scientists educate the media in interpreting social research.

and structural and political problems require structural and political remedies.

A few of the proposed solutions have to do with improving the formulation of research (see Figure 7). Prediction of research needs and improved strategies for planning research programs address the cognitive problems of research formulation. Unfortunately, both better prediction and better planning strategies are hopes rather than developed technologies at this point. Only modest steps have been taken to advance their capabilities.

The procedures for soliciting and reviewing research and for choosing appropriate research performers address structural problems associated with the location of researchers and the role of government staff and researchers. Attention to these factors is warranted, but there is not a great deal of reason to expect that future experience along these lines will be superior to the past. No one has yet invented another research institution like the Rand Corporation in its work for the Air Force, and the Rand Corporation's work for domestic agencies has not attained the same preeminence. Nor have there been any other breakthroughs that appear likely to satisfy equity and still lead to significantly more useful research. Still, there is modest potential in more effective matching of funding mechanism and performer to the research task at hand. Improvement is likely to come through the exercise of greater flexibility and the use of a larger number of options in initiating, developing, and funding research.

Better government monitoring of research has to do with the conduct of research rather than its formulation or application. To the extent that the attention of a project officer keeps the research from wandering off its appointed topic or helps the research adjust to up-to-the-minute shifts in policy concerns, it can be useful for maintaining relevance.

Stages of the Policy Research Process	Intellectual/Cognitive Domain	Social Structural Domain
From Policy Issue to Research Formulation	A Specification of the Research Problem Improved prediction of future needs Improved strategies for planning the research program	B Institutional Location of Policy Makers and Researchers Funding mechanisms Proposal review procedures Selection of appropriate research institutes and researchers
From Research Findings to Policy Implications	C Interpretation of Research Findings Inclusion of critical reviews of a study with a report Syntheses of previous research	D Application of Research to Policy Improved dissemination channels and procedures

FIGURE 7   Commonly proposed "solutions" to problems of research utilization.

Longer-range proposals, like better training of researchers for work in the real world and more emphasis on interdisciplinary research, might also make some contribution to research formulation and conduct. However, these ideas have long been espoused, and universities and research organizations have proved highly resistant to them. Small steps have been taken here and there, but there seems no likelihood of massive improvement.

Dissemination does seem to have greater potential for structural reform. It addresses the vital area of the application of research, the source of so many of the obstacles. Better mechanisms can be developed for linking research results to policy-making users. Three kinds of schemes are particularly impressive: (1) development of organizational channels for linking research to decision processes, especially through offices of planning and analysis; (2) disseminating integrated "state of knowledge" reviews of research rather than the results of one study at a time; and (3) using the mass media more effectively to report policy-relevant research.

Some obstacles are not removable by any of the "solutions" that have been the focus of discussion by government-oriented social scientists. None of those solutions is going to alter the fact, for example, that

- policy makers find it hard to identify research needs;
- agencies' stakes in policy bias the research they support and use;
- researchers formulate research in terms of the orientation of their discipline, their methodological expertise, and their social values;
- researchers and policy makers differ in orientation, conceptual bases, and styles of thinking;
- much research will come to inconsequential and ambiguous conclusions;
- research generalizations are applied in concrete, particular, and changing situations;
- resource constraints and status quo proclivities limit the implementation of research that calls for fundamental restructuring, except perhaps under conditions of crisis; and
- research is only one input into the complex bargaining around ideas and interests that is called policy making.

Some of these problems are insoluble, in the sense that any solution would be worse than the problem it aims to solve. A democratic system does not want technocratic solutions imposed on decision makers; a pluralistic society does not want political controls on the freedom of research. The tension between policy making and research can be fruitful and creative. Nevertheless, there are some steps that can be taken to make the juncture between research and policy more effective. Before turning to those, let us look at the implications of the remedies mentioned above.

Increasing Federal Control

Almost all the proposals that have been advanced to improve the research-to-policy fit include tighter control by federal staff. Emphasis on in-house planning of research programs, revision of procedures for research solicitation and review, and closer monitoring of research by government staff all call for increased authority for government insiders. Even the establishment of dissemination links would strengthen government staff by giving them greater opportunity to select which research to communicate, to whom, at what stage of the life cycle of the issue.

A stronger staff hand in the research-to-policy process has much justification. Staff, particularly in strategic offices of planning, programming, and analysis, are knowledgeable about issues and motivated by the desire to get the best possible information to higher echelons. Since it is often their job to analyze present and proposed policy options, they are the front-line users of research. They can help set priorities for what research is needed to fill gaps, with what precision and what timing.

However, there are disadvantages in allowing federal staff to monopolize research decisions. First, when heavy control is exerted in-house, the atmosphere becomes close and stuffy. However creative staff may be, they can generate only a limited number of ideas and plans, compared with the wide-ranging array that open solicitation brings.

Second, staff operate within a bureaucracy that sets limits. They are subjected to pressures to stay within the bounds of acceptable philosophy and operational feasibility. They have to pay attention to immediate needs and to research that promises knowledge that can be used and implemented within existing institutional arrangements. Any research that seems to call for drastic changes in program, structure, expenditure, or philosophy is likely to be discarded as not feasible—or risk veto by administrators. Emphasis on the feasible is a corrective against the inconsequentiality of much academically originated research. Too close a match to the issues and values of the moment, however, leads to rapid obsolescence. When the policy debate shifts, overly narrow research is left behind. Research of broader scope and generalizability can be more practical in the long run.

Third, the Washington-bound perspective may be a handicap in gearing research to issues of salience on the local scene. Many issues on which the federal government sponsors research are resolved by state and local decision makers. In corrections, education, health, environmental protection, law enforcement, and many other fields, federal departments can set guidelines for use of federal money, but state and local officials make operating decisions. Other consequential decisions are made by practitioners, educators, professional groups, private firms, clients, and consumers. Federal research staff are not ideally situated to understand the kinds of research that will make sense to them.

Finally, not all government project officers and analysts function on the same high level of competence. As in every occupation, some are poorly informed and mediocre in talent. To give a small group of staff the final say over a large proportion of government research funds is to risk poor decisions of enormous magnitude. More centers of decision and more dispersed loci of authority protect against massive central mediocrity.

Many social scientists are wary about increased government control not only because it would limit their own autonomy, but also because it would constrict the scope of research. Too much is unknown to put all our eggs in "practical research"; only as the knowledge base of the social sciences increases do we develop tested theories about human behavior that can be applied to many situations. With better theory, we would less often need to scurry to do quick-order inquiries about each separate situation. We would have generalizations that could reasonably guide policy in diverse fields, for example, how to improve children's learning, how to increase the productivity of public-sector employees, how to control rising health-care costs.

Researchers tend to be remote from government policy debates, but they are concerned members of society. With a critical, open, long-range perspective, they have much to offer about the direction that social research should take. In Weber's terms, there is a difference between the scientist's ethic of principle and the official's ethic of responsibility. Both have much to offer (Weber 1967).

Furthermore, other groups and interests should be parties to the research-to-policy enterprise. To the extent possible, research should be funded at many levels of government and by sponsors of many kinds outside government. This is a way to overcome the inevitable constrictions and biases that adhere to any one narrow set of views. When the expense of research makes government the only likely funder, planners should purposefully canvass many groups for their perceptions of the policy issue and the questions in need of answers. There should be communication not only between government and the academy before research is begun, but also among government, social scientists, and other attentive publics.

"Relevant" research is research that answers the real questions of persons participating in decisions. The pivotal phase in developing relevant research is framing the questions. The most important choice is to decide: whose questions?

CONCLUSION

Now there are a substantial number of significant people in public life who regard the social sciences as a bright hope for solving the social problems of the world. These positive expectations are refreshing but disquieting if the expectations are for too much too soon. The social sciences do have a contribution to make to social practice but not so large a contribution as they will make if helped to develop properly. At this point in history, the magnitude of social problems exceeds the capacity of social scientists to solve them.

This is an apt perspective from which to survey the future. As Riecken (1967, pp. 102–103) observed, the social sciences provide no panacea.

Neither do the social sciences provide an objective, apolitical substitute for political negotiation. Lindblom (1968) takes this view to the extreme, suggesting that research is not a substitute for conflict but a tactic used in the play of power. Research does not avoid fighting over policy; it is a method of fighting. Certainly when it enters the policy milieu, research loses much of its dispassionate quality and, as discussed above, often becomes ammunition for one side or another.

Research evidence does sometimes serve to reduce conflict by narrowing the zone of uncertainty. It establishes which variables are implicated in outcomes, something about their relative importance, and the interrelationships among them. It keeps people from arguing about what actually is, and saves them time to deal with the issue of values—with what ought to be. Although it does not resolve the policy issue, it focuses debate more sharply on its problematical and value-related facets.

Research does not solve problems; it provides evidence that can be used by men and women of judgment in their efforts to reach solutions. It helps to establish the premises on which the debate shall take place, providing an orientation, a language of discourse, and a conceptual base for the discussion of policy.

What we come to is a distinction between the social engineering model of research use and the enlightenment model (Janowitz 1970, 1972). Researchers as social engineers are expected to answer specific requests for information and knowledge in a straightforward manner. They are expected to take the government's ends as given and to devise means to achieve them. Since research is planned, done, and transmitted, it is expected to be applied. If the process does not flow smoothly, people come away disillusioned with research or with the research-to-policy process.

However, it has become increasingly clear that ends and means are hard to sort out; not only do ends become means to other ends, but also means and ends inevitably interact. As Schultze wrote (1968, pp. 38–39) after his years in the Bureau of the Budget:

Not only do our social ends or values conflict, but being subtle and complex, they are exceedingly difficult to specify. We simply cannot determine in the abstract our ends or values and the intensity with which we hold them. *We discover our objectives and the intensity we assign to them only in the process of considering particular programs or policies.* We articulate "ends" as we evaluate "means." . . . No one can specify in advance the weight he attaches to traffic safety versus rapid transportation except when considering a specific traffic safety program and evaluating its particular impact on the transportation system. . . . We all are interested in reducing the crime rate, and also in preserving individual rights, but we can handle problems of the tradeoff between the two only when considering a concrete program which affects both these goals.

The enlightenment model, on the other hand, assumes that social science research does not so much solve problems as provide an intellectual setting of concepts, propositions, orientations, and empirical generalizations. No one study has much effect, but, over time, concepts become accepted. People begin to accept, for example, that the introduction of advanced technologies in developing countries often has negative social side effects. The notion comes into currency that prisons, however enlightened, are poor places for rehabilitating criminals.

Over a span of time and much research, ideas like these filter into the consciousness of policy-making officials and attentive publics. They come to play a part in how policy makers define problems and the options they examine for coping with them. As Wilensky noted (1967,

p. 13) about exposing business executives and government officials to social science perspectives:

> If it does not yield direct answers to their immediate questions, perhaps it does break through their cruder stereotypes, enhance their understanding of themselves and their organizations, alert them to the range of relevant variables, and make them more skillful in the use of experts.

Social engineering can operate within narrow limits at this time. Certainly improvements should be made so that research is better conceived, carried out, and applied and so that the domain in which research functions is broadened. Better research methods need to be developed. Research on research can yield knowledge of both successful avenues and dead ends. Society has high consensus on many social needs—improved education, better health care, reduction in crime, lower unemployment. On topics on which there is consensus, society needs to find ways of reaching solutions.

Problem-oriented research therefore is called for, but so, too, is basic knowledge about the origin and persistence of social problems and better conceptual insights about ways of reducing their toll. At this point in their development, "enlightenment" may be the wisest use of the social sciences.

Much policy-related research goes astray because it asks irrelevant questions or phrases the questions in unproductive ways. As indicated at the outset of this paper, how to increase the use of social research in policy making is only one way to conceptualize the problem. An alternative is: how can public policy making be improved, and what role can the social sciences play in that improvement? It may be that we have been concentrating too hard on the first formulation and not hard enough on the second.

REFERENCES

Alkin, M. C., Kosecoff, J. Fitz-Gibbon, C., and Seligman, R. (1974) *Evaluation and Decision Making: The Title VII Experience*. Los Angeles: Center for the Study of Evaluation, UCLA Graduate School of Education.

Barton, A. H. (1974) Problems of Applied Research: Some Examples from an Applied Research Bureau. Mimeo. Presented at ONR Conference on the Utilization of Applied Research, Greystone Conference Center, Riverdale, N.Y., November 29–30, 1973.

Biderman, A. D., and Sharp, L. M. (1972) *The Competitive Evaluation Research Industry*. Washington, D.C.: Bureau of Social Science Research, Inc.

Biderman, A. D., and Sharp, L. M. (1974) The Selection of Social Research Performers: Formulations from a Study of Competitive Procurements of Social Program Evaluation Research. Mimeo.

Caplan, N., and Nelson, S. D. (1973) On being useful: the nature and consequences of psychological research on social problems. *American Psychologist* March: 199–211.

Caplan, N., Morrison, A., and Stambaugh, R. J. (1975) *The Use of Social Science Knowledge in Policy Decisions at the National Level.* Ann Arbor: Institute for Social Research, University of Michigan.

Chinitz, B. (1972) The Interaction between Research and Policy. Paper presented at Joint Institute on Comparative Urban and Grant Economics. Windsor, Ont.: University of Windsor.

Cohen, D. K. (1975) The value of social experiments. In A. M. Rivlin and P. M. Timpane, eds., *Planned Variation in Education.* Washington, D.C.: Brookings Institution.

Coleman, J. S. (1972) *Policy Research in the Social Sciences.* Morristown, N.J.: General Learning Press.

Coleman, J. S. (1974) The Social Structure Surrounding Policy Research. Mimeo. Presented at ONR Conference on the Utilization of Applied Research, Greystone Conference Center, Riverdale, N.Y., November 29–30, 1973.

Consad Research Corporation (1973) Summary of Interviews Related to Information Concerning Departmental Procurement of Research and Evaluation. Contract No. HEW-OS-73-134 with the U.S. Department of Health, Education, and Welfare.

Cowhig, J. D. (1971) Federal grant-supported social research and "relevance": some reservations. *American Sociologist* 6 (Suppl.):65–69.

Donnison, D. (1972) Research for policy. *Minerva* 10(4):519–36.

Dreyfus, D. (1976) The limitations of policy research in congressional decision-making. *Policy Studies Journal* Spring 4(3):269–74.

Duncan, O. D. (1969) Social forecasting: the state of the art. *Public Interest* Fall (17):88–119.

Dye, T. R. (1972) Policy analysis and political science: some problems at the interface. *Policy Studies Journal* 1(2):104.

Glaser, E. M., and Ross, H. L. (1971) *Increasing the Utilization of Applied Research Results.* Los Angeles: Human Interaction Research, Inc.

Gouldner, A. W. (1970) *The Coming Crisis of Western Sociology.* New York: Basic Books.

Havelock, R. G. (1969) *Planning for Innovation through Dissemination and Utilization of Knowledge.* Ann Arbor: Institute for Social Research, University of Michigan.

Horowitz, I. L. (1971) *The Use and Abuse of Social Science.* New Brunswick, N.J.: Transaction Books.

Janowitz, M. (1970) *Political Conflict.* Chicago: Quadrangle.

Janowitz, M. (1972) Professionalization of sociology. *American Journal of Sociology.* 78:105–35.

Jencks, C., et al. (1972) *Inequality: A Reassessment of the Effect of Family and Schooling in America.* New York: Basic Books.

Knezo, G. (1974) *Government Science Policy: Some Current Issues on Federal Support and Use of the Behavioral and Social Sciences.* Congressional Research Service for the House Committee on Science and Astronautics. Washington, D.C.: U.S. Government Printing Office.

Lazarsfeld, P. F., Sewell, W. H., and Wilensky, H. L., eds. (1967) *The Uses of Sociology.* New York: Basic Books.

Lindblom, C. E. (1965) *The Intelligence of Democracy.* New York: Free Press.

Lindblom, C. E. (1968) *The Policy-Making Process.* Englewood Cliffs, N.J.: Prentice-Hall.

Lipset, S. M., and Ladd, E. C., Jr. (1972) The politics of American sociologists. *American Journal of Sociology* 78:67–104.

Lynd, R. S. (1939) *Knowledge for What? The Place of Social Science in American Culture*. Princeton: Princeton University Press.

Lynn, L. E., Jr. (1973) A federal evaluation office? *Evaluation* 1(2):57.

McCrone, J. D., and Hoppin, M. E. (1973) Requests for proposals and universities. *Science* 179:175–77.

McDill, E. L., McDill, M. S., and Sprehe, J. T. (1969) *Strategies for Success in Compensatory Education: An Appraisal of Evaluation Research*. Baltimore: Johns Hopkins Press.

Merton, R. K. (1949) The role of applied social science in the formation of policy: a research memorandum. *Philosophy of Science* 16(3):175.

Merton, R. K., and Lerner, D. (1951) Social scientists and research policy, pp. 282–307. In D. Lerner and H. D. Lasswell, eds., *The Policy Sciences: Recent Developments in Scope and Method*. Stanford: Stanford University Press.

National Institute of Mental Health (1971) *Planning for Creative Change in Mental Health Services: A Manual on Research Utilization*. DHEW publication no. HSM 73–9147. 2 vols. Washington, D.C.: U.S. Government Printing Office.

National Research Council (1968) *The Behavioral Sciences and the Federal Government*. Washington, D.C.: National Academy of Sciences.

National Research Council (1969) *The Behavioral and Social Sciences: Outlook and Needs*. Report of the Behavioral and Social Sciences Survey Committee. Englewood Cliffs, N.J.: Prentice-Hall.

National Science Foundation (1968) *Knowledge into Action: Improving the Nation's Use of the Social Sciences*. Report of the Special Commission on the Social Sciences. Washington, D.C.: National Science Foundation.

Orlans, H. (1969) *Making Social Research Useful to Government*. Reprint 155. Washington, D.C.: Brookings Institution.

Orlans, H. (1971) The political uses of social research. *Annals of the American Academy of Political and Social Science* 384:28–35.

Orlans, H. (1973) *Contracting for Knowledge*. San Francisco: Jossey-Bass.

Pettigrew, T. F. (1973) Symposium on Jencks's "Inequality." *American Journal of Sociology* 78(6):1527–32.

Riecken, H. W. (1969) Social sciences and social problems. *Social Science Information* 8(1):102–3.

Roberts, M. J. (1974) On the nature and condition of social science. *Daedalus* 103(3):47–64.

Rose, R. (1974) Housing objectives and policy indicators. In *The Management of Urban Change in Britain and Germany*. London: Sage.

Rule, J. B. (1971) The problem with social problems. *Politics and Society* 2(1):47–56.

Schultze, C. L. (1968) *The Politics and Economics of Public Spending*. Washington, D.C.: Brookings Institution.

Sherwin, C. W., and Isenson, R. S. (1967) Project Hindsight. *Science* 156 (June 23):1571–77.

Sherwin, C. W., et al. (1966) First Interim Report on Project Hindsight. Summary. Defense Documentation Center. June.

Smith, B. L. (1966) *The Rand Corporation*. Cambridge, Mass.: Harvard University Press.

Smith, M. S. (1975) Evaluation findings in Head Start Planned Variation. In A. M. Rivlin and P. M. Timpane, eds., *Planned Variation in Education*. Washington, D.C.: Brookings Institution.

Stanley, D. T., Mann, D. E., and Doig, J. W. (1967) *Men Who Govern: A Biographical Profile of Federal Political Executives*. Washington, D.C.: Brookings Institution.

U.S. Commission on Civil Rights (1967) *Racial Isolation in the Public Schools: A Report*. Washington, D.C.: U.S. Government Printing Office.

U.S. Commission on Government Procurement (1972) *Summary of the Report of the Commission on Government Procurement*. Washington, D.C.: U.S. Government Printing Office.

U.S. Congress. House (1967) *The Use of Social Research in Federal Domestic Programs*. Committee on Government Operations. 4 vols. Washington, D.C.: U.S. Government Printing Office.

Weber, M. (1967) Politics as a vocation. In H. H. Gerth and C. W. Mills, trans. and eds., *From Max Weber*. New York: Oxford University Press.

Weiss, C. H. (1970) *The Consequences of the Study of Federal Student Loan Programs: A Case Study in the Utilization of Social Research*. New York: Bureau of Applied Social Research, Columbia University.

Weiss, C. H. (1972) *Evaluation Research: Methods of Assessing Program Effectiveness*. Englewood Cliffs, N.J.: Prentice-Hall.

Weiss, C. H. (1973) Where politics and evaluation research meet. *Evaluation* 1(3):37–45.

Weiss, C. H. (1974) What America's leaders read. *Public Opinion Quarterly* 38:1–22.

Weiss, J. (1976) Using social science for social policy. *Policy Studies Journal* 4(3):234–38.

Wilensky, H. L. (1967) *The Failure of Intelligence: Knowledge and Policy in Government and Industry*. Reprint No. 301. Berkeley: Institute of Industrial Relations, University of California.

Williams, W. (1971) *Social Policy Research and Analysis* New York: American Elsevier.

Wirt, J. G., Lieberman, A. J., and Levien, R. E. (1974) *R&D Management: Methods Used by Federal Agencies*. Santa Monica, Calif.: RAND Corp.

Young, P. V., Schmid, C. F., and Rice, S. A. (1939) *Scientific Social Surveys and Research*. Englewood Cliffs, N.J.: Prentice-Hall.

Social Science
and Public Policy:
A Personal Note

JAMES Q. WILSON

This paper reflects my own experience with governmental use of social science.[1] By "social science" I mean both carefully stated theories about human behavior and carefully tested propositions about such behavior; I do not mean simply the opinions of social scientists. I have not observed the full range, or even a fair sample, of governmental responses to social science. Those that I have observed directly include reactions to social science propositions about crime, drug abuse, and urban and campus riots; I also know, indirectly, something about governmental responses to pornography, family structure, and economic regulation.

The first and most important general observation I derive from these experiences is that only rarely have I witnessed serious governmental attention being given to serious social science research. That, of course, is what anyone would expect who is familiar with the maintenance and enhancement needs of bureaucratic organizations. I will make an even stronger statement: I have only rarely observed serious

James Q. Wilson, Harvey Lee Shattuck Professor of Government at Harvard University, is a distinguished social scientist with wide experience as an advisor to government.

[1] The contexts in which these observations were made include: (1) consulting with presidential commissions (those on crime, civil disorders, violence, campus unrest, and drug abuse); (2) analyzing the published reports of commissions to which I was not a consultant (that on pornography); (3) observing firsthand the reaction in agencies to social science claims (police departments, the Drug Enforcement Administration); and (4) reading about and talking with participants involved in the issues of family structure and economic regulation.

social science being presented to government agencies. If the latter is true, then the lack of any serious governmental response to social science is explicable on grounds quite different from organizational imperatives: there is nothing to which a response can or should be made. I suspect that in fact both mechanisms—organizational needs and social science inadequacy—are at work simultaneously.

Let me try to support my initial generalization. President Johnson asked the National Advisory Commission on Civil Disorders (the Kerner Commission) to discover "the basic causes and factors leading to" civil disorders. Chapter IV of the report of the commission (1968) gives its answer: "white racism" is "essentially responsible for the explosive mixture" that is then "ignited" by local incidents. Such racism has had three effects: segregation, black migration to big cities and the white exodus therefrom, and impoverished ghettos. One would suppose that there would be evidence that, not only have these social forces been at work, but that they have led to disorders.

There is no such evidence, at least on the latter and fundamental point. Indeed, evidence later gathered by social scientists casts serious doubt on this causal explanation. Studies sponsored by the commission itself suggest that the attitudinal component of the argument was specious: white attitudes toward blacks had become more, not less, benign in the years preceding the increase of violence; roughly the same proportion of whites as blacks endorsed racial violence, but only blacks participated; blacks who believed violence was an appropriate response to ghetto conditions were found as frequently in cities without violence as in cities with it; whites by a good majority favored governmental action to improve the lot of blacks (although they differed with blacks as to the cause of their plight); and so on. Perhaps all this could be interpreted in a way consistent with the commission's conclusion, but no such effort was made.

(Later research analyzing the conditions prevailing in cities with and without riots suggests that the more violent cities differed chiefly from the others in that they had more blacks. Income inequalities, on the other hand, were not systematically related to violence.)

On the single most important question facing it, the commission did not systematically gather and weigh such facts as were available. There is no sense in the report of a consideration of alternative explanations.

The National Commission on the Causes and Prevention of Violence, on the other hand, produced fifteen volumes of (in some cases) interesting research, took a long time perspective, and suggested that more than one factor might be a cause of America's persistent pattern of violence. When it came to policy recommendations, however, the commission based them on unexamined causal premises, untested ideas, and unstated facts.

For example, its first major recommendation, to "increase annual general welfare expenditures by about 20 billion dollars" as soon as the Vietnam War ended, implies that more welfare expenditures will purchase more domestic tranquillity and that inadequate expenditure in the past had caused domestic violence. It does not take "social science research" to cast some doubt on those propositions. If the commission had bothered to look, it would have discovered that in the two years immediately preceding the release of the commission' report, total social welfare expenditures had already been increased by more than $20 billion (actually, $28 billion). Such expenditures had doubled during the 1950s, nearly tripled during the 1960s, and they are well on their way to increasing in this decade at a far faster rate than that which the commission urged. Does anybody believe that we have less crime as a result? Or that collective violence, now much diminished, is less frequent today because of those increases?

The violence commission recommended that television broadcasters and the motion picture industry use greater restraint in presenting violence to audiences that include children. The commission found that "the preponderance of available research evidence strongly suggest . . . that violence in television programs can and does have adverse effects upon audiences—particularly child audiences." The great bulk of the research relied upon by the violence commission consisted of laboratory studies, usually involving young children or college students, in which "aggression" or "violence" was defined (in the case of young children) as a willingness to engage in harmless play activities involving physical force used on inanimate objects or (in the case of college students) as a greater willingness to administer ostensible electric shocks to other subjects under circumstances such that the student had no choice *whether* to administer the "shocks" but only how many and with what severity. It was never shown that what transpires in harmless play will later be transferred to interpersonal situations or that the laboratory experiments involving college students in any way simulated a reality in which the individuals could choose voluntarily to perform what they believed to be deliberate acts of violence against other persons.

The obscenity commission recommended repeal of federal, state, or local laws prohibiting the sale, exhibition, or distribution of sexual materials to consenting adults. It found that "extensive empirical investigation . . . provides no evidence that exposure to or use of explicit sexual materials plays a significant role in the causation of social or individual harms such as crime, delinquency, sexual or nonsexual deviancy or severe disturbances." The obscenity commission's effects panel did note the limitations of its research findings—long-term effects could not be investigated by a commission with only a two-year existence; there were almost no studies of the effects on children; and the behavior of volunteer (i.e., self-selected) subjects in experiments could not be generalized to any known population. Nevertheless, the effects panel drew attention to these findings when taking the view that there are no damaging personal or social effects from pornography.

Criticizing the banal and unsubstantiated policy views of public commissions is easy sport and I should be ashamed to indulge in it at the public's expense. I do so only to make a simple point: public commissions, on the record, have either made no use of social science (the Kerner Commission), made some use but in ways irrelevant to its policy conclusions (the violence commission), or made use of relevant but unconvincing and inadequate research (the obscenity commission). I have explored these matters in more detail elsewhere (see Wilson 1971, 1974).

Public commissions, especially ones appointed in a crisis atmosphere or dealing with emotionally-charged issues, are obviously ill-suited to the careful development and use of good research. Of course. Public commissions of this sort are powerfully induced to take positions, whatever the facts, that sound like (and usually become) editorials in the *New York Times*. Exactly why this should be the case is, to me, a far more interesting question than whether social science research was useful in getting to those positions. In my experience, it was not, but then I suspect that, under most circumstances, social science research is not very useful for getting to any position. I am struck by the fact that, on any given topic that has become a crisis, the amount of extant, policy-relevant, well-done social science research is just about zero. Social scientists offer their advice to these commissions, but their advice is rarely the product of research.

Suppose we try to get such research done and used in an atmosphere free of crisis and without the need for instant acceptability by an elite. These more relaxed conditions may help but alone are insufficient to produce the desired result. Daniel P. Moynihan began his research on the family structure of blacks out of personal curiosity, not in response to a critical event. He wanted to know why blacks so often failed the selective service tests. In answering that question, he discovered the high number of female-headed households among blacks and the apparent relationship between that fact and various social pathologies, especially crime and delinquency. He then proposed a "national effort" to enhance the stability and resources of the black family.

What followed is well known and the subject of numerous books and articles. President Johnson, desirous of setting a new direction in dealing with the race problem that would move beyond legal guarantees of civil rights, made the Moynihan view his view and the Moynihan language his language. In this situation, apparently, social science insights found an important sponsor at precisely the right moment. Mr. Johnson pronounced a presidential blessing on the Moynihan ideas with a speech at Howard University. For a moment, all was bright and serene; then the roof fell in. After acrimonious public and private debate, the permanent government—the higher civil service—and key White House aides more or less explicitly repudiated the Moynihan view. Note that they did not refute it; they repudiated it. To this day, no significant public official will raise the issue, although developments since then have made the initial argument even stronger.

What happened is easily explained. The Moynihan study was thought to imply (it certainly did not say) that blacks, alone or primarily, were responsible for their plight. It did say that ending white racism would not by itself cure that plight. Organized groups as well as spokesmen for unorganized groups were able to denounce any study that did not place the blame for black problems squarely and wholly on what was later (in the Kerner Commission report) called white racism. Furthermore, the study itself was vulnerable on some points (for example, its historical account of the breakdown of some black families would have to be revised in light of more recent knowledge) and lacked any clear policy prescription. The study could not say (in retrospect, it is not clear anyone could have said) what governmental actions would enhance the stability of the black family. There was, thus, no policy to be debated, only an idea to be considered—or to its critics, a slur to be denounced.

A second example of social science's gaining presidential support but losing the political war was the effort by economists early in the Kennedy administration to rationalize the policies of various regulatory commissions. They were able to convince key White House officials, on the strength of research that since has been reconfirmed and amplified in a dozen ways, that the regulation of rates charged by interstate common carriers was imposing unjustified costs on the consumer and creating inefficiencies in the industry. President Kennedy proposed to Congress that some changes be made—modest, first-step changes—to improve consumer welfare. His ideas died with their delivery. The Interstate Commerce Commission, the agency whose behavior was to be changed, was naturally opposed; so were many parts of the transportation industry that would have experienced more competition and less protection.

These two governmental rejections of social science findings that were generally correct should be contrasted with the governmental embrace of a social science theory that at the time had almost no evidence to support it whatsoever and that, when put to a test, was found wanting. In the Kennedy administration, the attorney general led a new federal effort to combat juvenile crime. There was at that time a new theory about the causes of delinquency developed by Richard Cloward and Lloyd Ohlin from the earlier work of Emile Durkheim and Robert Merton. It argued, briefly, that delinquency occurred when young people, denied legitimate means to attain legitimate ends, adopted illegitimate means to those ends. The means available were determined by the structure of opportunity available at the community level, a structure that could be altered, and thus improved, by community organization. This idea became the organizing principle for a number of important, publicly supported projects, notably Mobilization for Youth in lower Manhattan, which in turn became a partial model for the "community action agency" approach to dealing with poverty under the Office of Economic Opportunity.

At the time the theory carried the day, neither Cloward nor Ohlin claimed it was more than a theory. But it had the virtue that, true or not, it served the political and organizational needs of a variety of key actors: it seemed to be addressed to delinquency prevention; it appeared to get at the "root causes" of crime; it did not involve reliance on the allegedly stigmatizing and punitive effect of the criminal justice system; it could draw on the experience and enthusiasm of social workers and community organizers; it placed the blame for crime on "the system" and not on the juvenile; it provided a model for direct federal intervention in cities without relying on state governments and existing bureaucracies; it appealed to various foundations willing to put their own money into the effort; in addition to reducing crime, it would help mobilize communities to more effectively cope with local bureaucracies; and it might be a way of coordinating and monitoring the delivery of a variety of public services to the poor.

The pilot project, Mobilization for Youth, did a number of things about which there still swirls some controversy. About one thing there is no controversy at all: it did not reduce juvenile delinquency. Indeed, because of the multiple motives of those who organized the program, testing the potential of community organization to reduce delinquency was never a central goal of the effort.

There are contrary examples. Sometimes a major policy decision is made on the basis of little, if any, social science research, but, unlike the delinquency prevention example, the results seem to be beneficial and the process of carrying out the program stimulates research that, had it existed in the first place, would have supplied a justification for the program. Consider the case of drug abuse. President Johnson's crime commission (The President's Commission on Law Enforcement and Administration of Justice) essentially avoided the issue. President Nixon appointed no commission but did get some White House staff work done and solicited the advice of an energetic practitioner, Dr. Jerome Jaffe of Illinois. Simultaneously, Dr. Robert Dupont began, with help from a key senator and other federal officials, to introduce a methadone maintenance program in Washington, D.C., patterned after the work of Drs. Dole and Nyswander in New York City. Meanwhile, the State Department persuaded Turkey to try to stop farmers from growing poppies. The full story of these events has not yet been written, but certain things seem clear. First, there was no good analysis that would demonstrate either the relationship between heroin addiction and crime or the likely consequences for addiction of cutting off the Turkish opium supply by a crop-eradication program. Second, the crime-reduction potential of methadone maintenance did have some scientific support, though later analyses were to cast doubt upon it. Third, the effects of large-scale methadone distribution had not been tested.

Nevertheless, the White House committed itself to a program of reducing heroin supplies (by crop eradication and domestic law enforcement) and vastly expanded federal support for facilities in which "multimodality" treatments would be available but in which methadone would play a large—in many jurisdictions, a dominant— part. All of these programs become controversial. A subcommittee of the President's Science Advisory Committee criticized the Turkish opium ban because, it said, substitute sources could easily be found. Experiments in Brooklyn raised questions about how crime-free addicts using methadone had become. Many critics argued that law enforcement was raising the price of heroin and that, since demand for it was inelastic, higher prices would only lead to more crime, not less heroin consumption. Other critics claimed that methadone was no different from heroin: one addiction was being substituted for another.

After a few years, new research and more experience began to be

vailable that put these controversies into perspective. The demand for
eroin turned out to be somewhat price-elastic, so that as price goes up
arply, consumption drops. In certain regions of the country, alterna-
ves to Turkish-based heroin were much harder to develop than was
riginally supposed by the President's Science Advisory Committee;
ere was thus a net reduction in supply that endured for some time.
Iethadone lost its status as a glamour drug that would "cure" addic-
on or end crime and came to be seen, more realistically, as a useful
chnique for stabilizing otherwise willing addicts so that they could
spond to other treatment techniques (vocational assistance, training,
c.).

In short, my view is that the combined supply-reduction and
ethadone-treatment approach was on the whole a good idea. If it had
ot been tried when it was, the critical moment would have passed and
would then have become impossible. If there had been any delay for
ore extensive social science research, not only would the moment
ave passed but also the preliminary results of that research would
ave prematurely and unfortunately discredited the approach. A little
it of knowledge can be either a dangerous thing or a useful thing,
epending on the circumstances.

My last example involves local police departments. Contrary to
opular impression, police administrators are remarkably open to
hange—the problem is that they often make bad changes. They are
pen because their job requires them to prove that they are "doing
omething" about crime, corruption, narcotics, and community rela-
ons and not just "sitting there." They can make many changes stick
ecause of the strong, hierarchical personnel controls at their disposal,
lthough those controls have of late been eroded by police unionism
nd legal constraints. There is even an identifiable cycle of police
hange: tighten and centralize the organization to deal with corruption,
ecentralize it to deal with community relations, then recentralize it to
eal with riots or more corruption, specialize it to deal with crime, then
especialize it to create a "generalist" approach to crime, then
specialize it when the generalist approach does not work, and so on.
one of the changes are evaluated. The Law Enforcement Assistance
dministration seemed willing, alone or through its state planning
gencies, to pump money into almost any project, whether or not they
arned if it worked.

Of late there has begun a small movement to make planned, evalu-
ted changes in policing. The Kansas City Patrol Experiment, carried
ut jointly by the Kansas City Police Department and the Police
oundation, is the most conspicuous example. There are comparable

experiments under way on crime solution (Rochester), field interroga-
tion (San Diego), decentralized neighborhood policing (Cincinnati)
and one-man versus two-man patrol cars (San Diego). There have also
been some failures at this: I will spare the cities involved the embar-
rassment of mentioning them by name.

If planned, evaluated experiments are to be carried out, certain
things must happen. First, top administrators must genuinely want
them to happen and be willing to accept the risk that things may not
turn out as they would wish. (The Kansas City patrol experiment cast
doubt on the value of random, preventive patrol in marked cars. The
police chief who took office after these findings were published then
had a tough time explaining to his political superiors why he still
wanted more resources and a bigger budget.) Second, the operating
personnel of the organization must participate to some important
degree in designing and carrying out the project; they can easily
sabotage or ignore what they think is being imposed on them against
their better judgment. (In Kansas City, task forces containing officers
of all ranks worked on designing and running the experiments. This
was less so in other departments, but even there more personnel were
involved than just the members of some planning and evaluation unit.
Third, the experiment must be directed at some problem that is
important to both the organization and the community and must satisfy
the needs of those who do the work. (In Kansas City, the projects that
never got off the ground were those hatched in secret and carried out
over union opposition, which threatened pay and promotional opportunities, abolished valued specialities, or aroused community hostility.) Finally, there should not be, at the time the experiments are
undertaken, a powerful demand that "something be done" regarding
the ends toward which the experiment was directed.

Even with all these conditions met, there is still no assurance that the
results of an experiment will alter governmental behavior. The political
problems of the Kansas City police chief have already been mentioned.
In addition, the very process of carrying out an elaborate, well
designed, highly participatory experiment may partially incapacitate
the organization for further changes. In the Kansas City Police Department, there has been for a while a kind of paralysis resulting from
the conviction that nothing should be done that is not first verified
experimentally; since this is very costly and time-consuming, the
organization's ability to make even minor changes is reduced. By the
same token, others in and out of the organization may become convinced that the experiment is not worth the effort and resist further
efforts at change. The Kansas City experiment was greeted with two
kinds of responses from other departments: either "we already knew

hat" (in which case, why were they acting otherwise?) or "it's all wrong" (but without any serious evidence or argumentation to support he denial). Finally, many communities, eager to reduce crime, may press the department to extend new methods citywide before their value has been demonstrated in an experimental area, thus ending the possibility of experimental control.

From these reflections, I derive the following unscientific and nonexperimental inferences about the conditions under which social research and development has some chance of providing beneficial results to government.

(1) Getting good social science research is different from consulting good social scientists. The latter, unless watched carefully, will offer guesses, personal opinions, and political ideology under the guise of "expert advice."

(2) There are only a few occasions under which the requisites for social science research exist in the problem to be addressed. One must be able to solve the "index problem" (developing an unambiguous, reliable, and valid measure of the important and valued inputs and outputs); one must find a sufficiently large and unbiased sample of comparable cases such that reasonable statistical certainty exists; and one must somehow control for other variables, either statistically or experimentally. Many governmental problems do not meet these conditions.

(3) The best kind of social science research is the independently evaluated, controlled experiment. I stress "independently"—I know of few, if any, cases in which operating agencies can be trusted with evaluating the results of their own efforts. I also stress "experiment"—causal inferences from cross-sectional or even longitudinal data are very tricky; trying something to see if it works is far better. Often that is not possible, either ethically (we won't, I assume, experiment with alternative rates of capital punishment, for example) or economically.

(4) Good social science research, especially including evaluated experiments, requires the collaborative effort of the head of an agency, key subordinates, the affected operating personnel, and outside analysts and evaluators. The Kansas City patrol experiment had this. So also have the studies, sponsored by the Federal Power Commission and stimulated by outside economists, on the deregulation of natural gas prices.

(5) Such research also requires ample lead time, ample resources, and an absence of a crisis atmosphere or a polarized, attentive public.

(6) Items 2, 3, 4, and 5 taken together suggest that good social

science will rarely be used by government agencies in a timely and effective manner. Most organizations change only when they must, which is to say, when time and money are in short supply. Therefore, most organizations will not do serious research and experimentation in advance. When they use social science at all, it will be on an ad hoc, improvised, quick-and-dirty basis. A key official, needing to take a position, respond to a crisis, or support a view that is under challenge, will ask an assistant to "get me some facts." The assistant will rummage about among persons who are reputed to be expert, who are perceived to be politically sympathetic, and who are available at the moment. The process may take a few weeks, it may be done in a few hours. Social science is used as ammunition, not as a method, and the official's opponents will also use similar ammunition. There will be many shots fired, but few casualties except the truth.

(7) The resource in shortest supply in the development of good programs is not good research, but wise, farseeing, shrewd, and organizationally effective administrators.

REFERENCES

National Advisory Commission on Civil Disorders (1968) *Report of the National Advisory Commission on Civil Disorders.* Washington, D.C.: U.S. Government Printing Office.

National Commission on the Causes and Prevention of Violence (1969) *To Establish Justice, to Insure Domestic Tranquility.* Washington, D.C.: U.S. Government Printing Office.

Wilson, J. Q. (1971) Violence, pornography, and social science. *The Public Interest* 22(Winter):45–61.

Wilson, J. Q. (1974) Crime and the criminologist. *Commentary* 58(7):47–53.

U.S. Obscenity and Pornography Commission (1970) *Report of the Commission on Obscenity and Pornography.* Washington, D.C.: U.S. Government Printing Office.

Strengthening
the Contribution of
Social R&D to
Policy Making

HOWARD R. DAVIS *and*
SUSAN E. SALASIN

INTRODUCTION

SETTING THE SCENE

As Hegel might ask, does the transfer of social R&D into policy actually have its moment? If so, can its moment be so inglorious?

It is one of those sleepy Monday mornings in the office of a minor bureaucrat—typical of those so far to the lower right on the pyramidal table of organization on the office stationery that his name does not quite come out on the copies. Hoping that the tardy 8:30 A.M. appointment doesn't show up, he straightens his socks and listlessly goes over a document on his desk for clearance.

New legislation pertaining to community mental health centers must be followed by federal regulations on implementing the provisions of the act. After participating for many months in the development of the portion of the regulations dealing with program evaluation, he is about to sign when his eye catches these words: "Client outcome will be evaluated by assessment of the client's adjustment at a predetermined

Howard R. Davis, Chief of Mental Health Services Development Branch at the National Institute of Mental Health (NIMH), is a pioneer in the fields of research utilization and planned change. Susan E. Salasin, Chief of Research Diffusion and Utilization Section at NIMH, is the founder and editorial director of *Evaluation* magazine. The views expressed in this paper are those of the authors and not necessarily those of the National Institute of Mental Health.

93

follow-up point." Casually, his pencil drops to that statement and marks it out, substituting: "Client outcome will be measured by assessing the reduction of the client's presenting problem."

The change is so slight that it would hardly be noticed as a policy decision. But if the draft successfully runs the gauntlet through the Department of Health, Education, and Welfare (HEW) and public review to implementation, it ultimately will influence practice at community mental health centers throughout the nation in serving an estimated five million clients each year.

What the vignette illustrates are two attributes of policy making that confound any attempt at a systematic study of how social R&D contributes to policy in the mental health area. First, it illustrates that policy making is not just a presidential decision on whether the answer to unemployment is to stimulate the economy or to support public service job programs; it is not just a congressional decision on whether health care should be financed through private insurance companies or directly through the government; nor does it stop with cabinet members' decisions about the programs of their individual departments. Second, it makes clear that the moment when social R&D results are translated into policy is often silent, perhaps even unrecognized as such by the decision makers themselves.

The problem has been likened to Rabindranath Tagore's story of the holy man who wandered the roads, searching for the touchstone of truth. At first he examined each pebble with care, then in a more perfunctory way; as the years passed, he would pick up a pebble, touch it to his waist chain, and discard it without a glance. One day in gazing at his chain he was astonished that it finally had turned to gold. So he must have held the touchstone in his hand, but when and where he knew not.

In contemplating the unwalled and untamed nature of the knowledge-into-policy process, one might well assert that any discussion of how to improve it is likely to be imprudently bold. The assignment is not unlike trying to shackle a tornado. But the grave significance of policy making for the well-being of the nation's people, plus a sense of sharing some responsibility for ensuring optimum benefits from social R&D investments, moves us toward such an attempt, although necessarily with a strongly personal flavor.

Systematic study of the policy relevance of social R&D is imperative. Policy making may be viewed as the quintessence of government. Its effectiveness depends, at least in part, on policy makers having an understanding of policy issues and alternatives sufficient to allow them

» predict and control the consequences of the policies they adopt. This
pe of understanding is the ultimate objective of science. In our view,
)und governance occurs when the policy-making process seeks out
nd assimilates the clarification and predictability afforded by science.
 et our survey of the literature leads us to estimate that fewer than one
 ten papers on research utilization are addressed to questions con-
erning policy relevance. Surely such questions are more important
 an the meager attention devoted to them to date would suggest.

EFINITIONS

he following definitions of the principal concepts we use in our
iscussion may help in identifying our particular perception of the
 atter. Following *Webster's New Twentieth Century Dictionary*, we
efine "policy" as "any government principle. plan, or course of
ction" and "practice" as "the doing of something, often an applica-
on of knowledge."

We call attention to the distinction between policy and practice,
ecause inferences about the use of research in policy decisions will at
 mes be generalized from what already is known about its use in
 ecisions concerning practice, a subject on which a sizable literature
 ists. Such generalizations must be taken with caution; the significant
 ifferences between the phenomena of research into practice and
 search into policy are only under early investigation. It is likely that
 nowledge must pass quite a different entrance exam to gain admission
» the hurly-burly world of policy making.

According to the National Science Board, "research and develop-
 ent" comprises both basic and applied research. The aim of basic
 search is fuller understanding of the subject; the aim of applied
 search is potential applications of the acquired knowledge. We
 xtend this definition of research and development to include virtually
 ny use of scientific methods to produce policy-relevant knowledge.
 ur definition, for example, encompasses program evaluation. In the
 ray area are the many in-house derivations of knowledge that Caplan
 1975) has found to be predominant as sources of knowledge for policy
 akers.

Other definitions include: "dissemination"—the act of sending in-
 ormation on its way; "diffusion"—the spread of awareness of knowl-
 dge; "contribution"—with reference to social R&D, the direct influ-
 nce of knowledge on a specific policy decision as well as conceptual
 fluence on the policy decision.

THE VIEW OF THE POLICY MAKER

EVIDENCE ON RESEARCH USE

Caplan *et al.* (1975) have carried out what may be the most thoroug
study yet undertaken of policy makers' responses to social R&D. The
interviewed 204 persons from the White House, federal departments
and research institutes; 450 separate instances of the use of social R&I
in policy making were cited. The authors concluded (p. 4):

Many of the reported instances involved creative and strategically importar
applications of policy-relevant social science information and would sugges
reason for modest satisfaction rather than the despair and cynicism so preva
lent in the literature on the topic of social science utilization and nationa
policy.

These findings give reason for hope that systematically acquire
knowledge does find its way into policy.

However, the large proportion (51 percent) of respondents wh
included in-house sources and knowledge gained through newspaper
and other public media in their definition of social R&D give cause fo
some doubt. Research reports may have only modest impact on polic
decisions; information conveyed through familiar and trusted source
and not labeled as research is usually more influential.

Moreover, it may be important to learn not whether the responden
could name any instance in which social R&D had been used, but i
what percentage of decisions did such knowledge prove relevant. On
would hardly expect a policy maker to answer, "No, I don't us
knowledge in making any of my policy decisions." What would be th
results if the questions were asked in a different way, for example, "O
all the decisions you make regarding policies, in how many have yo
used social R&D results?" or "What percentage of the complete
researches on social R&D that you have observed have led to polic
formulation at any level?" Salasin and Kivens (1975, p. 43) posed
similar question to a former assistant director in the Office of Manage
ment and Budget, asking "What is your impression about the extent t
which evaluation findings, the outcome of analytic studies, were use
in reaching decisions about programs?" His answer was "It woul
be difficult in many cases to attribute more than five percent of th
ultimate changes that are made to any analytic contribution what
soever."

Besides endeavors such as the study by Caplan *et al.*, firsthan observations can give us a feel for consequences and help further our understanding of the social R&D "client." Richardson (1972, p. 16) offers one example regarding evaluation research:

study of the National Defense Education Act loans to students who undertake a career in teaching suggested that this had not been a significant incentive. It was possible to conclude, with the concurrence of the Congress, that the feature should be eliminated, and it was.

Lynn (1972) gives additional examples of HEW's use of evaluation studies of major programs, ranging from evaluations of the use of health-care services to an array of educational assistance programs. Effective use of studies among federal agencies was also reported by Riecker (in an unpublished document, 1974). In reviewing the roles played by social scientists working for the National Advisory Commission on Civil Disorders (Kerner Commission), Lipsky (1971) concluded that, in addition to their research contributions, the social scientists played an important role in legitimizing nonresearch staff reports.

Other observations and findings have not been so encouraging. In studying 350 policy and program changes at mental hospitals, Roberts and Larsen (1972) found that only 60 percent of them had been stimulated by research reports, with another 15 percent using research reports to refine decisions already made. Coleman *et al.* (1966) found that research reports influenced decisions to use a new drug in only seven percent of the instances. Of course, the decisions to use a new drug may represent a phenomenon far different from that of a policy decision. However, even while maintaining caution about overgeneralization from research on innovation, we still find it interesting that the Coleman *et al.* findings—namely, that research reports as such have only modest impact—have been replicated by many subsequent studies on information transfer. It is usually personal contact that is the influential factor. In the case of information on a new therapeutic drug, it was the sales representatives for the pharmaceutical house who influenced physicians' decisions in 57 percent of the cases. Could it be that "detail people" might be of assistance to policy makers?

It is not uncommon for social R&D projects to be carried out after policy decisions have been implemented in order to evaluate the consequences. Such studies have considerable potential for influencing subsequent decisions, particularly if the original policy makers remain interested and involved. But they can draw fire. Some people are inclined to look on post-policy studies as self-justifications. For example, when the National Institutes of Mental Health (NIMH) participated in a collaborative research grant to study the impact of the Lanterman-Petris-Short Act in California,[1] a volley of criticism came from groups involved in operating community mental health programs upon which the act had considerable influence. Their apprehension was understandable: The principal investigator was the former research director for the California Assembly, the individual who had carried out the staff work in drafting the act. The NIMH grant was looked upon as a device to be used by the assembly to stave of attempts to have the act repealed, despite evidence that control against bias had been carefully built into the research design. (As a matter of fact, one of the findings brought to light the deplorable circumstances endured by patients who were returning to the community under the act. The findings uncovered by this research project led to widespread reconsideration of such policies and the development of community programs to improve the lot of seriously mentally ill people.)

Those of us involved with producing and peddling social R&D information would like to believe that it should be the core of every policy decision. But that idea does not match up with reality. In an earlier experience one of us "lived" through a day with the top administrator of a state mental health program. At that level one makes at least subpolicy decisions daily; not infrequently, they amount to major changes in direction. The notion was that with our access to veritable silos of research and local statistical information, briefings could be provided for each encounter involving policy decisions. In hindsight, the outcome should have been obvious: in practice, decision makers must rely on their intuitive awareness of what will work and what will not and that determinants other than research information need to be taken into consideration.

More recently, an attempt was made to provide a division director in a federal program with analyses of data that would be helpful in making daily decisions, some of them policy decisions. A bright and eager person with a strong research background, he was highly motivated to make use of any available, relevant knowledge. In analyzing his calendar indicating various decisions that would arise during the week it became clear that our previous experience with the state administrator would repeat itself. Again, the division director's general awareness of relevant factors would serve him just as well as detailed analyses. Other actors involved in the decisions, what their bents might

---

[1] The Lanterman-Petris-Short Act modified the criteria for involuntary admissions to mental hospitals and altered the process for controlling mental health funds in the state.

be, changing circumstances that would impinge on the decision out-come, resources required to follow up the decision, and the losses and gains if one direction is taken over another are all relevant factors to be considered by decision makers. Even major program policy decisions would not necessarily be appreciably refined by specific qualitative and quantitative information. We are not saying that, as in Caplan's study, there are not notable instances in which social R&D results are used; if our experience is at all representative, however, the frequency of such instances among all policy decisions is low.

TWO WORLDS

The Institute for Community Studies once tried bringing together lead-ing social scientists and top administrators of human services programs in the Greater Kansas City area. The idea was to have the social scientists and policy makers engage in a dialogue for three days in order to exchange knowledge about agency problems with knowledge derived from research and to consider problems of designing processes that would extend social science contributions to policy. As lunchtime drew near the first day, many of the administrators began to disappear one by one—explaining that they "just had to get back to their offices for a while"—never to be seen again.

Despite the disappointing showing at this meeting, some interesting data had been gathered while the meeting was getting under way. Participants were asked to complete semantic differential scales that involved placing a mark on a line between opposite adjectives. They were to place the mark according to how they viewed administrators and again, with the same list of opposite adjectives, how they viewed researchers. Stereotype notions were confirmed. Researchers rated administrators as dedicated, hard-working, less bright than them-selves, and not to be trusted in the use of scientific findings. Adminis-trators viewed researchers as bright, lofty, and unconcerned about real-life problems. These descriptions would suggest that policy mak-ers and scientists do indeed live in two worlds.

A finding from the work of Caplan *et al.* (1975) further illustrates the difference between administrators and social scientists. Of national-level policy makers, 88 percent agreed with the statement (p. 28): "A major factor affecting utilization of social science knowledge is a lack of mutual understanding and interaction between the social scientists' community and the policymakers' community." Orlans (1969, p. 155) suggests: "To achieve . . . understanding, each side will have to give something: academics, the assumption that insight and intelligence (almost everything of value, indeed, except money) are largely on their side; officials, the notion that intellectuals, like supplies of office equipment, can be managed with contracts and money.''

An additional lesson may be learned from the meeting convened by the Institute for Community Studies. When the administrators slipped out, they might have been demonstrating that administrators prefer a world of action and immediacies to that of intellectualizing. They might have been saying that they felt intimidated by some of the nation's eminent social scientists. If the scientists had singly visited an administrator's "turf" and talked policy language rather than research language, would the scientists have been more successful?

Knowledge may be an unwelcome intruder into the world of policy. Green (1971, p. 15) notes:

The policymakers' world is the familiar one of incremental change and political prudence; the world in which one proposes nothing startlingly innovative until the last possible moment, so as to avoid making enemies and mobilizing centers of resistance.

It is unfair to generalize about all policy makers, but Campbell (1973, p. 402) provides a warning:

Ambiguity . . . and lack of concrete evidence . . . work to increase the administrator's control over what gets said, or at least to reduce the bite of criticism in the case of actual failure. There is safety under the cloak of ignorance.

The decision maker who turns to research runs the risk of losing freedom in making choices, unless the research supports a position he or she wishes to take. Once one is confronted by research-derived, cogent solutions to a problem, the only options open are to use it or to ignore or abuse it. Were the early attacks on sociologist James S. Coleman really because of the statistical techniques he used or because of the startling—and, in the national media's version, unqualified—finding that school inputs had almost no effect on achievement, a finding that puts educational policy makers in an awkward position?

Weiss (1973) reminds us that in establishing policies, the key proponent may have invested far more in the takeoff than in the landing. This is particularly true in the world of public policy, where turnover among top officials is taken for granted. Furthermore, the outcome of a major policy or program decision may be diffuse and difficult to ascertain. The policy maker may be poorly motivated to make the effort needed to acquire detailed information for refining a program. Policy makers have a need for social R&D contributions, but need in itself is not a motivator; only felt need is. It would seem negligent to depend on the better mousetrap theory and assume that if social R&D builds a better policy, policy makers will naturally beat a path to the researcher's door.

THE VIEW OF THE SOCIAL R&D COMMUNITY

A REVIEW OF COMPLAINTS

It is not only the behavior and attitudes of policy makers that frustrate the efficient production and use of social R&D results. One can recite a litany of valid complaints about the social R&D community.

The first is that researchers have not been eager to employ social research tools in studying the effectiveness of social R&D. As Orlans (1973, p. 197) said, "A type of evaluation that has been singularly lacking has been the evaluation of the quality and effectiveness of social research programs themselves." It is not only lack of interest that inhibits the scientific study of the use of knowledge. From our own experience, we are convinced that methods of tracing the careers of R&D findings are staggeringly difficult to develop. It is as though knowledge flows through underground rivers, which branch and rejoin one another in complex ways. When the rivers break the surface, it is almost impossible to trace their origins.

We made an initial attempt to evaluate the use of results of R&D projects in mental health about 10 years ago. We discovered that for only 1 in 10 projects that had been completed for at least a year could any use of the findings be identified at sites other than the project site. However, we doubt that these findings are directly relevant to assessing the policy relevance of social R&D. Perhaps the last thing one should do in studying policy relevance is to study the use of research project by project. Further our criterion of use dealt not with the use of social R&D in policy making, but with its impact on clincial practice, a much easier phenomenon to measure.

A second set of complaints centers around the reluctance of social researchers to work on specific policy problems. Riecken (1971, p. 100) said, "Social scientists have found it advantageous to ally themselves with physical scientists in seeking support, with one result being the encouragement of empirically-oriented research rather than politically controversial topics." A similar view was expressed in the report of the Rockefeller Foundation Conference on the Social Sciences in Rural Development (Rockefeller Foundation 1976, p. 15):

The academically motivated social scientists tend to select problems and solutions that fit into their own research designs, and these are seldom useful to national or agency policy. For example, economic research is often under-utilized by people making operational decisions because it is too tied to the dicipline's theories and pays insufficient attention to institutional problems.

Williams (1971) believes that, of the many "macronegative" studies (e.g., "Blacks and poor"), too few address specific policy solutions.

Our empathy with social scientists makes it understandable to us that they are reluctant to be drawn into policy debates. Framing research in terms of national goals often means that the results will not get published in academic journals and thus earn university promotion. Archibald (1968) points out that researchers who simplify and gener-alize their results to make them useful to policy makers often earn only contempt from their academic colleagues. Williams (1971, p. 63) con-cludes that:

. . . the important social scientists who play for the highest stakes in the social science community—particularly peer prestige—do not dirty their hands much with that which is relevant to social policymaking. Those who do such work are almost assuredly of lower caste.

The researcher does not always realize that he or she is wading into dangerous waters at the time of launching research. The awareness may not come until years later. One might consider, for example, the experiences of Jolyn West and Margaret Singer, who have done work on brainwashing. Their research was innocuous when it was done, but later they were asked to testify in the Patricia Hearst case. It would seem they were morally bound to express the views derived from their research in that instance. In so doing, it also gave them an extraordi-nary opportunity to expand awareness and enlightenment about the distinctions between brainwashing and coercion, and their contribu-tions could eventually lead to modified social policies.

Not all researchers readily take to the function of effectively promot-ing the diffusion and use of their own findings, although some are superb, and notable names are easy to recall (for example, Amitai Etzioni or Thomas Kiresuk). However, there are many social R&D scientists who have abundant ability to participate in diffusion and use (beyond dissemination through academic journal publication) and who prefer not to become involved because of notions about the cultural values in the scientific community; that is, values implying that it is as improper for scientists to purvey their own findings as it is for profes-sionals to advertise. We feel there is no reason such people, if genuinely unwilling, should be pressed into these activities. Perhaps this is another reason for reflecting sympathetically on the advisability of having specialist brokers, such as policy analysts, involved in the knowledge-into-policy process.

A third set of criticisms is directed at federal research managers like ourselves. It may be that some of us in federal agencies that fund social R&D projects join with academe in reducing incentives for scientists to engage in policy-relevant research; some of us are no closer to the world of policy than are those in academic institutions. Would we really recognize and reinforce features of proposals specifically designed to render the work more relevant to policy?

Federal research managers face additional constraints. Even though agencies may give full endorsement to program efforts to develop technologies in the use of research and to promote policy-relevant research, as is certainly true within the National Institute of Mental Health, research managers also rely heavily on outside review and advisory groups. When those groups are inclined toward more traditional research, it makes it difficult to offer consultation to researchers to help them get their proposals successfully through the review gauntlet. Research design consultation becomes more difficult as the problem under study encompasses more of the diffuse real-life problems that do not lend themselves to scientific control as influencing variables. Thus, some research managers tend to favor the development of proposals that contain tidy designs for studying narrow topics because the review may go much smoother that way.

Another management problem is that designing project provisions that will enhance the probability of policy relevance takes money: using representatives of policy makers as observers or consultants in the early planning phases, extending data collection to multiple sub-samples of persons or factors, issuing publications and holding conferences to stimulate policy makers' interest in ongoing research and results—all take added funds.

In the hope of guaranteeing further funding, some research managers try to yield nice, crisp findings that are easy to communicate and have interest appeal. Having such findings to report at budget hearings is what may count in retaining budget allocation levels. This means that even though we, as bureaucrats, carry the responsibility of optimum impact for research investments, we may unwittingly reduce relevance and place social scientists in a second jeopardy of shifting their research from the problem at hand to one with greater popularity.

A final set of complaints has to do with the quality of social R&D. There appears to be little more work on evaluating the quality of social

R&D than on the use of research results. One recent exception to that is the evaluation of research supported by the National Science Foundation (NSF), carried out by a committee under the auspices of the National Academy of Sciences. Of particular interest to the social R&D community are the conclusions of the committee on NSF's program on Research Applied to National Needs (RANN). RANN was launched a few years ago with much hope that through its valiant efforts it could bring the potential contributions of applied research to meet the needs spanned by its five major divisions: energy, environment, productivity, intergovernmental science and public technology, and exploratory research and problem assessment. In the judgment of the committee (National Research Council 1976, p. 77): ". . . the quality of work is highly variable and on average relatively undistinguished, with only modest potential for useful application."

The committee felt that the programs are not enlisting as wide a range of participation from the social and behavioral science communities as could be expected. The committee felt that it would help if the structure of the RANN programs were recast to correspond more closely with the applied social science disciplines and if more responsibility for program planning and problem definition were placed on members of those disciplines, working closely with representatives of potential user groups.

Bernstein and Freeman (1975) did not confine their disappointment about the quality of research to one agency. After auditing evaluation research in the Departments of HEW, Labor, Justice, Housing and Urban Development, Agriculture, the Office of Economic Opportunity and NSF, they chose this statement for the final sentence in their book (p. 152): "For considerable cost, current evaluation research seems to be failing to live up to its promise."

It would be unfair to leave this consideration of the quality of social R&D in a mood of despair, however. There are abundant sound findings produced by hosts of able and skilled social scientists. Even if the policy yield from these research investments appears small, we are enthusiastic about what can be done to increase that yield.

In a study carried out by Glaser and Taylor (1969), some 100 projects that had terminated in the previous year were evaluated. Outcomes at both tails of the distribution (high quality and low quality) were matched on the basis of topic, investment of funds, and duration. The reviewers, operating without awareness of which project in a pair was rated high or low, carried out in-depth discussions with a number of people who had been associated with each project. Also, the original applications for the projects were analyzed and coded by factors.

Results revealed that 15 factors differentiated the matched high-quality and low-quality projects. The resulting scale for assessing proposals was cross-validated with a subsequent year's yield. The scale accurately predicted the outcome in approximately 80 percent of the proposals.

Interestingly, none of the factors had to do with the industry or earnestness of the investigator, though past performance of the scientist did serve as a predictor. Most of the factors pertained to variables that could be improved through consultation and providing potential investigators with information. Evaluation of comparable projects over the years has confirmed that without great wrenching of existing values or traditions, the quality of research and development can show remarkable improvement. A documented outline (U.S. Department of Health, Education, and Welfare 1971) summarizes most of the advised techniques.

BARRIERS TO QUALITY

On the basis of formal evaluations and experiences in the management of some $150 million in mental health R&D investments, we would like to offer our impressions of seven barriers to maximum quality of R&D.

The setting in which a project is carried out may not be harmonious with the outcome desired. R&D grants are awarded to researchers in both operating agencies and academic settings. When the grantee institution is an operating agency, the policy and practice relevance of the outcome, not surprisingly, is more likely to be assured. When the grantee institution is an academic one, the scientific validity and generalizability of the new knowledge gained tend to be greater. Operating agencies gain more from the federal grant in either learning more about their own situation or inaugurating a trial innovation; at the same time, research rigor is a lower priority. In the academic setting, on the other hand, the investigator's incentives usually include the chance of meeting with referees' approval so that one can publish and build professional capital. It might be said that social R&D scientists working for an operating agency must watch their "Ps and Qs"; in the academic setting, investigators must watch their "sigma and beta weights." Blending the two has proved to be very difficult.

Cross-validation of findings in different settings with varying populations is seldom carried out. Replications are expensive and are not highly valued by those who approve research proposals because "it's already been done." Investigators themselves gain only a small increment of advantage by investing extensive time and effort in replications. Publication already will have occurred. Since most researchers are by nature inventive, few wish to launch a study simply to replicate someone else's work. They may have trouble getting such work published.

Good policy-relevant research now calls for a technology that extends considerably beyond expert awareness of the substantive area and skill in research design. It calls for sophistication in formal needs assessment; knowledge retrieval and convergence; involvement of potential users through collaboration, consultation, and selection of relevant criterion measures; use of new data-collection and analysis methods; integrating research process with diffusion and use activities (not just dissemination); and the use of follow-up evaluation over time.

Persistence in the imposition of classical experimental design allows the results to be generalized only to narrowly focused and controllable problems. (We hope the monumental work of Guttentag and Struening [1976] will foster the use of more appropriate methods in social R&D.)

At the federal level, the evaluation of both quality and consequences of research and development is too infrequent. In addition, there is insufficient evaluation of review criteria as well as the review process to ensure fidelity between approval and the quality and consequences of research.

Again at the federal funding level, there is insufficient awareness in preparing for effective collaborative relationships between research consultants and managers on the one hand and scientists and policy makers on the other. Even though many federal staff members have been social R&D researchers or users, they tend to drift away from the skills and perspectives of both. The sense of accomplishment and potential contribution in the role of facilitation, consultation, coordination, and guidance are sometimes forgotten in either the frenzy of pushing papers or the appeal of deep involvement in projects fitting one's own substantive interest. In fact, the failure to process papers well—put purely and simply—can break the federal research administrator faster than anything else. Not inappropriately, it tends to shape one's values and behaviors.

Perhaps above all, overload suffered by most federal research administrators and staff impairs the attainment of the best yield from the research enterprise. (Recently, in one research training grant program, three or four staff members were burdened with processing some 600 applications virtually overnight; funds were available for only 30.) Reviewers and advisers similarly are inundated with work in their valiant efforts to assist the federal agencies. Our evaluations have revealed that beyond-chance runs of disapproval recommendations tend to occur during the long evening hours into which the review process often has to extend.

The point is that the overload problem (and sometimes the arrogance that can overcome one in processing huge sums of money) can make us forget the critical importance of maintaining sincere respect and appreciation of investigators and what they are doing. Diplomacy and common courtesy on the part of research administrators—at all levels—are far more consequential in the ultimate benefits from the research enterprise than we sometimes stop to realize.

THE SOCIAL R&D PROCESS: SOME POSSIBLE MODIFICATIONS

In order to strengthen the social R&D contribution to policy making, we suggest a number of action steps or modifications under the headings of the policy process, the research enterprise, and the knowledge-transfer process. We hope that some may evoke enough interest to be examined either through evaluation of the need for change or through research that clarifies the issues. As is the case with policy making, decisions about process should be viewed with objectivity. As George Bernard Shaw once said, "If it is not necessary to change, then it is necessary not to change." Thus, the suggested modifications should be reviewed but not necessarily adopted without further thought and investigation.

THE POLICY PROCESS

Clarification of the Policy Process

Any sophisticated policy maker in a responsible position realizes the "anatomy and physiology" of the policy process, but social R&D investigators often lack that awareness. The policy process needs to be clarified; it must be analyzed and synthesized in a form that is readily communicated to researchers in a fashion that will promote assimilation of R&D results. Efforts should be made to enlist the support of policy makers, researchers on policy, and research funding agencies in sponsoring clarifying studies and in preparing materials that can be used by social R&D investigators.

Analyzing the determinants of policy decisions is a complex undertaking, but it is not unapproachable. As an example of a sapling model for analyzing the decision process, the Decision Determinants Analysis model developed by Davis (1973) is of interest. The DDA model (also referred to as the A VICTORY model) rests on the assumption that agencies, and the policy processes within them, are living systems, as pointed out by Leavitt (1965) and Shepard (1965). Processes within agencies are determined by the same factors that guide all human behavior. The factors that are held to be necessary in accounting for decisions are translated from theoretical jargon into eight terms: obligation, information, value, capabilities, circumstances, training, resistances, and yield.

• *Obligation*   Existence of a need for a decision in itself is insufficient to set the process in motion. Awareness of the need and felt pressure are necessary to motivate action. The greater the motivation and sense of obligation, the more likely the decision process will be carried out.

• *Information*   Knowledge of the terrain and familiarity with alternate courses of action must be considered by the social scientist in dealing with the decision process.

• *Values*   The goal of the agency, the philosophies and personal predilections of the decision makers themselves, authorities superordinate to them, key participants, and ultimate beneficiaries must be reconciled to the course chosen. The operating style of the agency, its history of policy establishment, and even its size and diversity may become silent selectors of alternative courses.

• *Abilities*   Decision alternatives should be guided by the agency's capabilities to implement the chosen alternative through funds, personnel, and, above all, its own power to invoke an option.

• *Circumstances*   Existing conditions, often beyond the control of the agency, that shape or limit the alternatives must be considered. New legislation, public outcries, investigation revelations, evaluation findings, or change of administration may represent circumstances that evoke and shape decisions.

• *Timing*   Closely allied with circumstances is the consideration of what is going on at the moment. Crises, for example, may influence the alacrity of the decision-making process.

• *Resistances*   Often unspoken unwillingness by persons involved in the decision process may alter its course.

• *Yield*   Every decision rides on the assumption that the outcome will be salutary, a problem resolved, or progress gained. Social R&D can be critical in predicting the yield from alternative decisions.

As is evident, these factors interact. From the standpoint of social R&D, each factor is open to study as it relates to a given policy issue. In research that deals with testing alternative courses of action, such as social experimentation, all factors, not just yield, should be considered part of the evaluation. The following incident illustrates how the role of each factor can be detected in a decision situation.

In the early days of interest in mental health patient aftercare, NIMH invested heavily in research on techniques to reduce the likelihood that discharged patients would have to be rehospitalized. It was found that a very simple practice contributed greatly to reducing rehospitalization: a social worker from the patient's county of residence visited the hospital, established a working relationship with the patient, and participated in planning for discharge prior to the termination of hospitalization.

We proposed to the commissioner of public welfare that he adopt a policy of statewide implementation of this practice. The commissioner was responsible for the County Welfare Department, which in turn held legal responsibility for services to patients discharged from state mental hospitals. His department also had authority for the state mental health program, including the hospitals. Thus, he was a person with the prerogatives to adopt the policy. And since he was known for progressive administration, there had been little doubt that the commissioner would agree to adopting the practice. Surely he would be grateful for this simple way to reduce readmission rates.

But after listening to the proposed plan, he pushed his chair back, slowly lit up a cigar, and eyed us. Instead of leaping for joy at our proposal, he said he would like to ask a few questions. In essence, they were as follows.

How will people in our hospital social service departments feel about county workers coming in and taking over a major portion of what they have seen as their roles? And how will the counties feel about extending the duties of their employees beyond the responsibilities which they normally carry? [He was concerned with violating the assumed *values* of the system.]

In your project, you used experienced psychiatric social workers and public health nurses with masters degrees. How do I know that our county welfare workers will be able to match the skills of your project workers? How will we pay for the training programs necessary to prepare the county workers to carry out the same aftercare services? Where do I find funds to pay for their travel expenses to the state hospitals? Who will carry out the work that they will be unable to accomplish while they are spending the required time at the hospital helping the patients prepare for discharges? [The commissioner was asking about the *capability* to implement the policy.]

Your findings sound almost too simple and pat. How do you know the results you obtained did not stem from the skills of the workers on the project? And how do you know that their small caseload of only about six patients at any time wasn't the determining factor? [The commissioner was appropriately questioning the soundness of the *information* stemming from the research.]

In your project, your workers had their offices in the city very close to the hospital and the locations of the patients after discharge were also fairly close. There aren't many parts of the state where things are that convenient. Will the plan still be feasible? [The commissioner was suggesting that the *circumstances* would likely work against the success of the change.]

The counties aren't going to volunteer to use their scarce resources for added service unless legislative and budget adjustments are made. The state legislature just met. How will I bridge things throughout the rest of the biennium? [Clearly, *timing* had not been considered.]

Readmission rates are already respectably low. Who is so critically concerned about the problem that the increased expenditures would be warranted? Of course, I'd like to see readmission made unnecessary even for one patient, but it would help if the legislature, the governor, or at least some groups were concerned enough to back this policy. [The *obligation* to change was not pressing.]

The need for social workers in our hospital would be considerably less. Some may lose their jobs. How will I handle their unhappiness? And the county workers are going to be raising Cain because of the hardships they'll face, even if compensation is arranged; they will have to stay away from their families during trips to the hospital, for instance. [The commissioner was reminding us that *resistances* had been overlooked.]

Though your results are statistically significant, would the improvement in the readmission rate be sufficient even to be noticed? Will anyone feel better for having gone along with this policy if it should be adopted? [*Yield*, the reinforcing reward necessary to sustain successful change, admittedly was minimal.]

What we learned from this experience was that reality must be contended with in establishing policies and also that research findings are useless unless the full pattern of adoption determinants is considered in the research design.

Understanding the Policy Maker as a Client

It is axiomatic that the greater the knowledge about any client's perceptions, feelings, values, needs, and ways of operating, the better he or she can be served.

In analyzing data provided to the Continuous National Survey Experiment, which was a continuous polling of government agencies to determine problems about which they requested new information, Rich

(1975) found that policy makers who were involved in the decisions concerning what information should be collected were more likely to make use of the available information than those who were not. Caplan *et al.* (1975) reported that 85 percent of the national-level policy makers interviewed believed that social science knowledge can contribute to the improvement of government policies, but noted that most policy users call on the information to serve as a check on the validity of preexisting beliefs. Further, policy makers like to use information found in newspapers, allowing a feeling that their awareness does not lag behind others. The implications of such insights as these could be of valuable assistance to the inventive communicator of research knowledge.

Caplan *et al.* (1975) have offered further information that can be potentially helpful in planning transfer, or communication, efforts. He reported that policy makers discriminate among disciplines in their assumptions about the validity and reliability of the information communicated. For example, on a rating from 1 = good to 10 = poor, Caplan's respondents rated physicists at 2, economists at 5, sociologists at 6, political scientists at 7, and psychiatrists at only 7.6. Policy makers felt the most valid information was that obtained through observation in real life, then came surveys, followed by controlled field experiments. There was little confidence in information that came from experimental games and simulations. The policy makers relied heavily on newspapers, government reports, and staff papers. Just over half of their research information used came from in-house studies. Caplan said (p. 47) that ". . . only rarely is policy formation determined by a concrete point-by-point reliance on empirically grounded data."

From the standpoint of the policy maker, Caplan concluded that the use of social R&D is most likely to occur when the policy maker has a reasoned appreciation of both the scientific and extra-scientific aspects of the policy issue; the values of the policy maker carry with them a sense of social direction and responsibility; the policy maker has a clear definition of the issue and how research knowledge can contribute a solution.

THE RESEARCH ENTERPRISE

Coordination among Federal Funding Agencies

The lack of coordination among social R&D administrators in federal funding agencies can lead to costly, unintentional duplication of efforts in several respects, which may also limit the effectiveness of the agencies. A quasi-formal group of social R&D administrators could at least ameliorate some communication, coordination, and referral problems. Agglutinations of this sort have existed from time to time in Washington, but have flagged for lack of structure and clear purpose. Specific functions that such a group might have are: pooling efforts to maintain a high level of staff performance; pooling research knowledge and techniques, integrating interagency research funding; and serving as liaison between policy makers and scientists.

POOLING EFFORTS TO MAINTAIN A HIGH LEVEL OF STAFF PERFOR-MANCE A professional consortium of some sort could do much to reinforce motivation and keep scientific skills alive. Refresher programs could be provided in consultation skills, scientific progress in particular areas, new developments in research methodology, and the like. This would help bring about the opportunity to commiserate, exchange approaches, and maintain a high level of interest and professional self-esteem. Orlans (1973, p. 195) notes that "red tape, the circumspection required in public remarks, the need for loyalty to superiors, the obligation to implement and justify unwelcome policies, the exposure to congressional harassment, the constant pressures that reduce operational freedom without reducing personal responsibility . . ." represent deterrents to effective pursuit of the research administrator's work. With respect to evaluation, Bernstein and Freeman (1975, p. 136) add:

The various Federal groups have other functions. . . . Most of their "middle-management" cannot be expected to have the training and time, let alone the commitment, to initiate, monitor, and promote studies of outstanding quality. Their jobs are bigger than evaluation research, they must get them done.

Uyeki (1965) found that the most successful research administrators were those who had gained experience in research careers, who went into research management because they saw this as an opportunity to be influential in their chosen fields, and who continue to invest time in research.

POOLING RESEARCH KNOWLEDGE AND TECHNIQUES Knowledge is sorely needed on new design methods in social R&D, on methods of evaluating the quality of research and tracing its consequences, on processes of knowledge utilization, and even on the transfer of social R&D into policy. Most programs must be dedicated to topical problem matters. But beyond that barrier, benefits derived from independent research programs endeavoring to develop process knowledge could be generalizable across all social R&D programs.

INTEGRATING INTERAGENCY RESEARCH FUNDING   Some social issues are of such a magnitude and diversity that no agency's primary mission spans all facets of them. The investigator or research group who wishes to launch a comprehensive study has to build up a research operation piece by piece, with all the chance and frustration that involves. Agencies should integrate their systems and devise a procedure to render such projects more feasible.

SERVING AS A LIAISON BETWEEN POLICY MAKERS AND SCIENTISTS   As Rich (1975, p. 245) put it so well: "Researchers cannot know what the decisionmaker's agenda is by osmosis." Working with policy analysts, a consortium could collaborate with social scientists about current needs in policy research. One channel for such communication, which NIMH administrators have already put into operation, might be symposia at national meetings of social science disciplines. In order to encourage timeliness of research, formal events might be planned with observers of the social issues scene in which analytic and future techniques could be employed.

Flexibility in the Use of Funding Mechanisms

Most research administrators use few of the funding alternatives open to them in accomplishing program missions. A useful aid for administrators would be an inventory of the types of funding mechanisms used by various federal agencies. The two major mechanisms, of course, are grants and contracts.

Grants constitute the bread-and-butter mechanism of many research programs. Although the federal staff may cooperate in planning the study and its operation, the investigator remains boss, and federal influence is restricted to persuasion. The mechanism retains the important scientific independence of the investigator, yet can add measurably to the work and mission of an agency.

"Diffusion and utilization supplements" to awarded grants represent an innovative experiment in more flexible use of that mechanism. For projects that promise high yield in a priority area, the federal representative may request special efforts of the investigator. Because of the conditions in awarding the supplement, this action may result in a "hardship" to the investigator who receives additional funds through a grant supplement.

The small-grant mechanism, generally confined to projects funded at no more than $5,000 per year, offers the advantage of shorter lead time for pilot or exploratory endeavors. The period from submittal deadline to project approval is reduced from 6 or 7 months for regular grants to perhaps as short a time as 2 months for small grants. Contracts are actually purchases by the federal government for something it presumably wants; technically, the resulting product belongs to the government. Consequently, the mechanism implies constraints for the scientist. Perhaps for that reason, contracts to investigators are more commonly associated with private research firms. Contracts offer the advantage of shorter lead time, and the customary 1-year duration of supported projects yields faster results. In the past, contract proposals have been reviewed as much on the basis of low bid as on the quality of the proposal.

The short term from need to product, plus the opportunity to gain information that is critically needed for the mission of the agency, as in decision-planning for the forthcoming policy, makes the contract mechanism potentially a most valuable one. But two changes are needed. First, more social scientists should seek and work on such contracts. At present, social scientists may head the firms that win contracts, but too often turn over the execution of the research to less trained and experienced employees. Second, federal staff should be more involved in planning and collaborating on contract research.

Improvement of Quality

Users of mental health services research and development results are more concerned with the relevance of those results to their problems than they are with the scientific merit of the results. However, it is the responsibility of both investigators and research managers to ensure that any results reported meet the highest feasible standards.

With respect to extramural studies funded through grants and contracts in the federal government, Bernstein and Freeman (1975, p. 137) sum up their findings on what produces high quality:

Have all studies undertaken in academic research centers, by Ph.D. psychology professors and those with similar training and orientation, include a commitment that the research results must be published in refereed social science journals, provide funds only as grants and have them awarded on a basis of peer-review committee judgments, allow a time period of three to five years for the planning and conduct of research, have the grants monitored by Federal officials with a high degree of social science graduate training and with reference groups consisting of academic researchers, and insist on the research being undertaken in collaboration with the action agency.

But they hurriedly point out that there is more to policy research than hard-nosed methodological merit. Problems of delayed availability of results and their relevance to current policy matters are as important as standards of scientific merit. It appears that considerations must be more complex and research on policy relevance must go further.

Campbell (1969) deplores the pressure sometimes imposed on social researchers who work in close conjunction with policy-minded administrators. While recognizing that a truly experimental approach to social amelioration may be precluded, he urges social researchers to guard against nine specific threats to internal validity of their work, including regression artifacts that can occur when units have been selected on the basis of their extreme scores, selection biases resulting from differential recruitment of comparison groups, and the differential loss of respondents from comparison groups. Unfortunately, the classic Campbell and Stanley document (1966) setting forth quasi-experimental methods appropriate in social research remains ignored by many investigators.

For the conscientious investigator who adheres rigidly to experimental designs, he or she may end up doing more and more rigorous research on less and less significant problems. There simply are too many issues in social policy that do not lend themselves to effective control over extraneous variables. Guttentag (1973) advocates the use of the "decision-theoretical approach," which is rather new to social research, but based upon classical Bayesian techniques; it allows encompassing a broad range of natural social circumstances. In advocating this approach over classical experimental design, she points out that most social programs just do not lend themselves to the control of variables upon which the experimental paradigm depends. The method she is promoting tolerates the continuous incremental decisions that must be made during the course of a program.

One step toward upgrading the quality of social research may grow out of a new contribution by the Russell Sage Foundation. As a special section in *Evaluation* magazine, now distributed to nearly 50,000 readers, critiques of designs employed in federally sponsored social research and evaluation projects will appear regularly. The critiques, prepared by experts under the foundation sponsorship, should prove invaluable as guides to social R&D investigators in approving their own designs.

The Guttentag and Struening two-volume *Handbook of Evaluation Research* (1975) represents a milestone toward improving the quality of social R&D. The volumes span virtually every aspect of concern to social R&D investigators, including ethical, conceptual, and methodological ones. But it may be that a less intensive guidebook also should be prepared for early and quick reference by persons planning social research intended to be relevant to policy making.

Study of Review Processes

Peer reviewers and readers come close to constituting a nerve center of the research enterprise. They represent the top talent, by reputation, among the nation's scientists. And they should, considering their immense responsibility not only in giving key guidance to the investment of approximately a billion dollars each year but also, even more importantly, in determining what research efforts will yield the greatest benefits for all citizens. Funding agency staff develop a warm reverence and even a sense of personal friendship with review panel members, though committee decision prerogatives must never be infringed. In observing the role differentiations between reviewers and staff, some of us as federal research managers feel we have no responsibility to ensure that the decisions are reliable and valid as predictors of sound investments of citizens' dollars.

In order to let review committees know whether they are placing consistent emphases on certain factors from meeting to meeting, this procedure is used in NIMH: all comments made during the discussion of each project that reflect value implications, such as "I don't understand what the applicant is saying," are written down verbatim. Each is marked as to its negativeness or positiveness and also according to whether it was said about a project that has later been approved or disapproved. In the analysis phase, the comments are sorted by eyeball into clusters, such as "design," "budget appropriateness," and "clarity." A two-by-two table is prepared for each cluster. All comments that have a positive rating for reviewers' value intimations and also a plus sign for eventual approval recommendation are represented by a tally mark in the upper left cell. The other three possible combinations of plus and minus signs are distributed accordingly in the three other cells. If a given factor is a perfect predictor of the ultimate approval recommendation, then all tallies will fall in the upper left cell, which will contain all positive comments and approval recommendations, and the lower right cell, which will contain all negative comments and disapproval recommendations. This distribution is tested by a simple chi-square test. If the distribution is statistically significantly different from chance, then that factor is multiplied by the frequency with which it was mentioned during the three-day review process. The result is a weighting of decision determinants used during that particular round of reviews.

It may be of interest that, consistently, the most heavily weighted factor is clarity of the proposal. The second most heavily weighted is approach and research design. The third is usually the competence of the investigator. One factor that is almost always a perfect predictor, although not heavily weighted because infrequently mentioned, is evidence that remarks made during a site visit were responded to. Budget is discussed with great frequency but rarely does it show a significant relationship with approval or disapproval recommendations. Validity has been checked by determining whether priority ratings given for approved projects predict the quality of the research as judged by independent raters some time after termination of the project. Obviously, the wisdom of disapproval decisions cannot be checked because the projects are aborted.

Attracting Research Investigators

The quality of a research project is, to a significant degree, a function of the performer. Reviewers appear, correctly in our view, to place heavy weight on that factor. Encouraging the submission of proposals from people who can be identified as top performers has its pitfalls, however. It cannot be done at all, of course, with contract research—unless a "sole source" contract (for a situation in which only one performer has the qualifications needed to carry out the research) can be authorized. One has to be careful that favored help is not being given to one applicant that is not available for others, as would be fair in an open, competitive system. Also, even if a proposal is solicited from an outstandingly qualified investigator, there is still no assurance the proposal will meet with success in running of the review gauntlet. Still, some approach is needed to ensure that applicants include investigators who are in a position to do the best social R&D work.

In mental health R&D, psychologists are heavily involved. This is good to the extent that the use of research results is associated with that discipline. But if criteria of successful outcome are going to include the use of results by policy makers, investigators in other disciplines, such as political scientists, public administration professionals, and especially economists, must also be involved.

An approach needs to be developed to ensure that an optimum array of investigators are attracted to participate in social R&D. Perhaps increased awareness through use of specialized media would be better than individual solicitations.

New Models of Research

As things tend to be now, if an investigator with a good performance record in traditional terms submits a proposal with a clear and basic traditional research design, the probability is that the project will be approved for funding. But the proposal may characterize a project that has narrowed its focus to a topic that readily lends itself to classical design, that allows smooth collection and analysis of data, with results that are likely to be published in the refereed journals. And that's it: the results are interred on a library shelf and the world goes on struggling with its problems.

The following are some attributes that should characterize research in order to optimize relevance to policy.

Planning the research:

Anticipate crises, future needs for knowledge.
Identify potential users; solicit their consultation.
Gain understanding of user's needs.
Search literature for closest comparisons.
Anticipate long-range efforts, extending to diffusion and utilization procedures.
Plan for cross-validation.
Simulate user conditions.
Use adviser groups, representing both potential users and key communicators.

Designing the research proposal:

Ensure that findings will meet the test of the acronym, CORRECT:
Credibility—sound and convincing.
Observability—clear, demonstrable.
Relevance—expressed in terms meaningful to users.
Relative advantage—pointing to a decision that will improve a problem state.
Ease of understanding.
Compatibility with existing values.
Trialability, divisibility, or reversibility if results are tried in implementation.

Conducting the research:

Sensitivity to the environment (people) of project site.
User audience participation.
Regular reports, such as newsletters.
Conferences to acquaint communicators of progress.

Readable reports.
Participation in diffusion and adoption.

One major contribution to strengthening social R&D would be the development of a successful approach for cross-validation of findings. Investigators may be deluding themselves into thinking that a complex multivariate design will account for the interaction of all independent variables, i.e., the events that are likely to influence the outcome of interest. But what works in Hoboken may not work at all in Seattle. While that may not matter if the researcher is helping a policy maker in Hoboken, if there is a desire to lend generalizable results to a national policy, it matters very much indeed. If social R&D findings are to be generalizable they will have to be replicated in different settings. As we discussed above, there is resistance to this: review bodies are disinclined to award grants to repeat the same study; there are no incentives for a scientist to repeat research already done; and the costs involved in cross-validation experiments are high.

Open exchange of findings and interpretations through seminars would help to resolve conflicting interpretations and to expand awareness of issue factors. A 1975 *Washington Post* article reported on a seminar conducted by the Brookings Institution in which Martin Feldstein, a Harvard economist, produced widely disseminated studies suggesting that because a worker has unemployment insurance replacing about 65 percent of net pay, he or she stays out of work longer than if there were no such insurance. Inferences were made that unemployment insurance should be curtailed. However, during this seminar, Stephen T. Marston of Brookings pointed out that, based on other studies of the problem, although the unemployment insurance system does extend the average duration of unemployment, it is by such a small amount that we can stop worrying about it. The debate that took place at this meeting may have caused some policy makers to lose confidence in social scientists who disagreed so sharply in their conclusions on an important policy issue. Nevertheless, confrontations of this sort may be a real answer to the inevitability of inconclusive findings in social R&D.

Mission-oriented research centers, an idea originating with the natural sciences, could represent a solution to certain of the problems in applying social R&D findings to policy. An organization could receive support for a program of research projects, all focused on clarifying one broad social issue. The operation would be more than simply an instrument for a spate of related studies, however. Its resources would include functions ranging from continual formal assessment of knowledge needs, retrieval of existing relevant information and monitoring other ongoing researches, clarification of components of the issue or testing innovative solutions, diffusion and use of new knowledge for policy makers, and reevaluation of the original needs pertaining to the issue. Examples of such organizational research programs are the Rand Corporation's work with the Air Force and an NIMH-supported collaborative grant with the Mitre Corporation.

THE TRANSFER PROCESS

This paper has been primarily concerned so far with understanding the policy process and the policy maker. We now turn to actions or modifications that might be developed between the policy world and the research enterprise. Some of the actions are already in operation or have been tried. However, further research on actions such as these could lead to refinement rendering them still more helpful in bringing the two worlds closer together.

Support of Synthesizing Material

Documents, such as annual reviews and monographs, already exist that bring together new knowledge on given topics. Lateral dissemination of that sort of material is good and frequently used by other researchers. But vertical dissemination from researcher to practitioner and among potential users seldom takes place, according to Paisley (1969). Investigators working on common topics could be invited to participate in meetings to exchange findings and reports of progress. Not only could the content of new social R&D knowledge be considered, but also its implications for policy use. Policy makers or analysts could be invited to participate, affording a greater understanding of the utilization potential of the new knowledge. Progress reports on new knowledge could be prepared, again with emphasis on the aspects that would be most pertinent to its ultimate use in policy.

Gatherings of investigators in related fields are commonplace, of course. However, what we have in mind is a process structured deliberately toward considerations of policy use. Informal experiments on this approach have already been tried for the topics of operations research and change technology, with at least moderate success.

Information Retrieval Services

Obtaining information is really not a difficult task now; formal data systems abound. For example, some 2,000 articles related to mental health are abstracted and stored each month, and there are at least 15 major computerized services available that have pertinence to mental health. More generally, there are 20 indexes to the periodical literature and 16 review publications. There are commonly known deficiencies of retrieval systems: overabundances of information not highly related to the initial request; lack of screening of abstracts that will be included, allowing much inferior chaff in the yield; abstracts that are written to describe rather than to provide content; and so on.

Even with their deficiencies, such sources carry much relevant information for policy decisions. Easy-to-use directories are available to those motivated to seek information. But even when typewriter-sized computer terminals and microfiche readers are placed in the offices of potential users, the devices are not used. Scientists use automated retrieval systems, but policy makers rarely do. Perhaps continued research will find a way to overcome the apparent resistance.

The Invisible College

The network of informal contact between social scientists and persons in a position to influence policy probably accounts for far more transfer of social R&D results into policy than most of us realize. For example, James Q. Wilson's proposed solution on crime (that a minimum sentence be mandated for violent crimes and that judges be required to impose them) showed up in a speech on crime by former President Ford. One can gain a vague impression that its use may have resulted from Wilson's personal reputation and obvious contacts. When sociologist Peter Rossi learned of relevant and convincing information pertaining to justice, he was quite free to send a note to his former colleague, former Attorney General Edward Levi.

Orlans (1973, p. 209) sums it up well: ". . . influence depends as much on perception, character, opportunity, acquaintanceship, persuasiveness, and powers as on the truth." Alas, little if anything is published to document what happens in the invisible college. It warrants research and evaluation for further use as a process, despite the maddening problems of analysis.

Policy Implication Papers

An innovative system was launched in HEW in 1971 in an attempt to bring the results of department-supported research to the attention of appropriate policy makers. As staff members became aware of research findings that had implications for policy improvement, they were to submit that information to the assistant secretary for planning and evaluation for further consideration. The procedure was simple in concept and was consistent with the findings later reported by Caplan *et al.* (1975) about the preference of policy makers for in-agency research information. The primary problem in the system's operation, however, was that researchers were unaware of opportunities for policy decisions within the department. But the idea has sufficient merit as an experiment, and it should be analyzed with the Decision Determinant Analysis method described by Davis and Salasin and then tried again. It represents one potential for helping to bridge the chasm between research and policy.

Specialized Media

Printed material has been used so extensively to disseminate information that one is wearied at the prospect of further experimentation with it. However, two experiments are currently under way to test the effectiveness of magazines designed to compete for reader attention and response. Analysis of *Evaluation: A Forum for Human Service Decision-Makers* has found that 36 percent of its readers report an actual change in policy or practices based upon information provided in the magazine. Because the magazine has a circulation of about 50,000, it is proving most effective as a means of conveying social R&D information. An evaluation of *Innovations: Highlights of Evolving Mental Health Services*, with a circulation of approximately 10,000, shows that 18 percent of its readers report actual changes that have taken place on the basis of information disseminated through the magazine.

Transfer Specialists

Effective dissemination of knowledge is an undeniable first step that must be taken in making social R&D results helpful to policy makers. As we have noted with the magazine experiments, some use of information does take place. But of the potential opportunities for matching relevant knowledge with appropriate policy processes, what proportion of those matches actually take place?

On the side of every pack of cigarettes, research findings are disseminated that tell the smoker, "cigarettes may be hazardous to your health." If there were ever well-disseminated research information, that is it. Yet cigarettes sales continue to climb each year. Surely something more than individual awareness of information determines its assimilation into behavior. It is a matter of the human condition: 1,940 years ago the Apostle Saint Paul lamented, "that which I would do I do not and that which I would not do I do." Whatever it was that Saint Paul was doing that he was not to do, and vice versa, he was not alone in his predicament.

A program of research is needed on the feasibility and effectiveness of transfer specialists. Their functions could include services as liaison and broker between social scientists and policy makers; retrieval and synthesis of relevant knowledge; technical assistance on assimilating knowledge into the policy process; and consultation on anticipating implementation as it might affect the policy-making process.

CONCLUSION

Our proposed modifications draw on a rather extensive literature on research use and change, plus field experiments with the use of information consultants. Until the measurement of the social R&D contribution to policy can be developed, implementing changes toward strengthening that contribution remains essentially an exercise. Again, we would underscore our advocacy of employing the tools of social R&D in meeting the opportunity to make policies of even greater benefit to the well-being of the people affected by them.

REFERENCES

Archibald, K. (1968) The Utilization of Social Research in Policy Analysis. Doctoral dissertation. Washington University.

Bernstein, I., and Freeman, H. E. (1975) *Academic and Entrepreneurial Research: The Consequences of Diversity in Federal Evaluation Studies.* New York: Russell Sage Foundation.

Campbell, D. T. (1969) Reforms as experiments. *American Psychologist* 24:409–29.

Campbell, D. T. (1973) Experimentation revisited. *Evaluation* 1(3):7–13.

Campbell, D. T., and Stanley, J. C. (1966) *Experimental and Quasi-Experimental Designs for Research.* Chicago: Rand McNally.

Caplan, N. (1975) A Minimal Set of Conditions Necessary for the Utilization of Social Science Knowledge in Policy Formation at the National Level. Paper presented at the Conference of the International Sociological Association, Warsaw, Poland.

Caplan, N., Morrison, A., and Stambaugh, R. J. (1975) *The Use of Social Science Knowledge in Policy Decisions at the National Level.* Ann Arbor: University of Michigan, Institute for Social Research.

Coleman, J. S., Katz, E., and Menzel, H. (1966) *Medical Innovation: A Diffusion Study.* New York: Bobbs-Merrill.

Davis, H. R. (1973) Innovation and change. In S. Feldman, ed., *Administration in Mental Health.* Springfield, Ill.: Charles C Thomas.

Glaser, E. M., and Taylor, S. (1969) *Factors Influencing the Success of Applied Research Results.* Final Report to the National Institute of Mental Health, Contract 43-67-1365. Washington, D.C.: U.S. Government Printing Office.

Green, P. (1971) The obligations of American social scientists. *The Annals* 394(March):13–21.

Guttentag, M. (1973) Subjectivity and its use in evaluation research. *Evaluation* 1(2):60–65.

Guttentag, M., and Struening, E., eds. (1975) *Handbook of Evaluation Research*, vols. 1 and 2. Los Angeles: Sage Publications.

Leavitt, H. J. (1965) Applied organizational change in industry: structural, technological and humanistic approaches. In J. G. March, ed., *Handbook of Organizations.* Chicago: Rand McNally.

Lipsky, M. (1971) Social scientists and the Riot Commission. *The Annals* 394(March):72–83.

Lynn, L. E., Jr. (1972) Notes from HEW. *Evaluation* 1(1):24–28.

National Research Council (1976) *Social and Behavioral Science Programs in the National Science Foundation: Final Report.* Committee on the Social Sciences in the National Science Foundation. Assembly of Behavioral and Social Sciences. Washington, D.C.: National Academy of Sciences.

Orlans, H. (1969) *Making Social Research More Useful to Government.* Reprint 155. Washington, D.C.: The Brookings Institution.

Orlans, H. (1973) *Contracting for Knowledge.* San Francisco: Jossey-Bass.

Paisley, W. J. (1969) Perspectives on the Utilization of Knowledge. Paper presented at the meeting of the American Educational Research Association, Los Angeles.

Rich, R. F. (1975) Selective utilization of social science related information by federal policymakers. *Inquiry* 12(3):239–45.

Richardson, E. R. (1972) Conversational contact. *Evaluation* 1(1):9–16.

Riecken, H. W. (1971) The federal government and social science policy. *The Annals* 394(March)100–113.

Roberts, A., and Larsen, J. (1972) Effective Use of Mental Health Research Information. Final Report. NIMH Grant No. R01-MH-15445.

Rockefeller Foundation (1976) The Role of the Social Sciences in Rural Development. Working papers, an interagency conference, New York, January 1976.

Salasin, S., and Kivens, L. (1975) Fostering federal program evaluation: a current OMB initiative. *Evaluation* 2(2):37–44.

Shepard, H. A. (1965) Changing interpersonal and intergroup relationships in organizations. In J. G. March, ed., *Handbook of Organizations.* Chicago: Rand McNally.

U.S. Department of Health, Education, and Welfare (1971) *Planning for Creative Change in Mental Health Services: A Manual on Research Utilization.* Washington, D.C.: U.S. Government Printing Office.

Uyeki, E. S. (1965) Behavior and self-identity of federal scientists-administrators. In Yovitts *et al.*, eds., *Research Program Effectiveness.* New York: Gordon V. Breach.

Weiss, C. H. (1973) Where politics and evaluation research meet. *Evaluation* 1(3):37–45.

Williams, W. (1971) *Social Policy Research and Analysis.* New York: Elsevier Scientific Publishing Co.

BIBLIOGRAPHY

American Institutes for Research. Innovations: Highlights of Evolving Mental Health Services. Supported by NIMH grant no. R12-MH-25121. American Institutes for Research, Palo Alto, Calif.

Behavior Today. The great debate. December 15, 1975, p. 639.

Coleman, J. S., *et al. Equality of Educational Opportunity.* U.S. Office of Education. Washington, D.C.: U.S. Government Printing Office, 1966.

Davis, H. R., and S. Salasin. The utilization of evaluation. In M. Guttentag and E. Streuning, eds., *Handbook of Evaluation Research*, vol. 1. Los Angeles: Sage Publications, 1975.

Etzioni, A. Non-conventional uses of sociology as illustrated by peace research. In P. F. Lazarfeld, W. H. Sewell, and H. L. Wilensky, eds., *The Uses of Sociology.* New York: Basic Books, 1967.

Etzioni, A. Revenue sharing five years later. *Washington Post*, April 4, 1976.

Glaser, E. M., Methods for Sustaining Innovative Service Programs. NIMH collaborative grant no. R12-MH-27566. Los Angeles: Human Interaction Research Institute.

Human Interaction Research Institute. Information Sources and How to Use Them. In collaboration with NIMH. Los Angeles: Human Interaction Research Institute, 1975.

Kiresuk, T. J., and S. Lund. Process and outcome measurement using goal attainment scaling. Pages 213–28 in J. Zusman and C. R. Wurster, eds., *Program Evaluation: Alcohol, Drug Abuse and Mental Health Services.* Lexington, Mass.: Lexington Books, 1975.

Larsen. J. Dissemination and Utilization of Information. NIMH collaborative grant no. R12-MH-25121. Palo Alto, Calif.: American Institutes for Research.

Light, R. J., and P. V. Smith. Accumulating evidence: procedures for resolving contradictions among different research studies. *Harvard Educational Review* 4(41):429–71, 1971.

Marx, M. H. *Psychological Theory.* New York: Macmillan, 1951.

Minneapolis Medical Research Foundation, Inc. Evaluation: A Forum for Human Service Decision-Makers. Supported through NIMH grant no. R12-MH-25619. Minneapolis: Minneapolis Medical Research Foundation, Inc.

National Institute of Mental Health. *Planning for Creative Change in Mental Health Services: A Manual on Research Utilization.* DHEW publication no. HSM 73-9147. Washington, D.C.: U.S. Government Printing Office, 1971.

National Institute of Mental Health. *Research in the Service of Mental Health.* Report of the Research Task Force of the National Institute of Mental Health. Washington, D.C.: U.S. Government Printing Office, 1975.

National Science Foundation. Science indicators 1974. In *Report of the National Science Board.* Washington, D.C.: National Science Foundation.

Rein, M., and S. M. Miller. Social action on the installment plan. *Trans-action* 3(2):31–38, 1966.

Salasin, S., Mental Health Research into Practice. Minnesota Department of Public Welfare Contract Report, 1968.

Salasin, S., and H. R. Davis. Evaluation: invitation to organizational change. In I. Davidoff, M. Guttentag, and J. Offutt, eds., *Evaluating Community Health Services: Principles and Practice*, in press.

Tiffany, D. W., P. M. Tiffany, and J. R. Cowan. The source of problems between social science knowledge and practice. *Journal of Human Relations* 19(2):239–50, 1971.

Time. Coleman on the griddle. April 12, 1976, p. 79.

U.S. Department of Health, Education, and Welfare. Secretaries' Research and Evaluation Guidance. Office of the Secretary. December 1971.

Weinberg, A. M. *Reflections on Big Science.* Boston: Massachusetts Institute of Technology Press, 1967.

Weiss, C. H. Organizational Constraints on Evaluation Research. NIMH contract no. 46-969-82. New York: Bureau of Applied Social Research, Columbia University, May 1971.

Research Brokerage:
The Weak Link

JAMES L. SUNDQUIST

At 10 o'clock on almost any weekday morning, the members of one or another subcommittee of the Congress will be assembling to write social policy into law—and to complain, in the process, that they do not have the basic information they need in order to do their job intelligently.

At the same time, in some university or research institute, there is likely to be a social scientist with at least some of the information the subcommittee needs—perhaps unaware that the subcommittee even exists, perhaps unaware of the pertinence of what he or she knows to what is going on in the world of public policy, or perhaps fully aware but simply frustrated that the information is somehow just not getting to those who are making policy. Or, if no researcher has exactly the information for which the subcommittee is searching, there is likely to be an investigator or team somewhere who could have assembled the necessary data with a little lead time and a bit of money.

Given this state of mutual frustration, the process by which social science knowledge gets from the producer to the consumer (assuming in this discussion the user is the federal government) is worth examining. This examination requires some caveats: it is based on unsystematic observation, it may repeat what others have said more authoritatively, and its generalizations are subject to the qualifications

James L. Sundquist, Senior Fellow at the Brookings Institution, is the author of *Politics and Policy* and numerous other books and articles on government decision making.

throughout that the pattern described is extraordinarily variegated and full of exceptions and special cases.

THE TRANSMISSION OF SOCIAL KNOWLEDGE

As the terms "producer" and "consumer" suggest—and as has been remarked by various writers—the transmission of social knowledge from the point of origin to the point of use in the policy-making process is akin to the marketing of physical goods—farm products, for example. The produce of the farm must be assembled, processed, packaged, and put on the right shelves at the right time. So must the products of social science research.

As in the marketing of physical goods, the producer of social science knowledge rarely deals directly with the consumer (in this case, the federal policy maker). There are exceptions—John Maynard Keynes once talked with Franklin D. Roosevelt—but such a situation is analogous to a farmers' market: not a very large proportion of agricultural produce is sold that way (nor is it clear that Keynes made a sale on that occasion). Agricultural marketing is the responsibility of a chain of intermediaries. So it is with the marketing of social science research.

In the system of knowledge marketing, two broad categories of intermediaries can be identified. At one end, dealing directly with the producers, are the gatherers, processors, and wholesalers of information—academic intermediaries, as it were. At the other end are the packagers and retailers who prepare and present the information in usable form to the policy maker who is the consumer: these are the staff units or individuals who serve Presidents, department heads, bureau chiefs, congressional committees, and individual members of Congress as links with the academic world. They carry many titles— economic advisers, research and statistics offices, policy analysts, legislative assistants, and many others. They need a generic title and "research broker" is as good as any. The flow of social knowledge can be diagrammed, then, as a movement from A to D through either, and usually both, of the intermediate points B and C:

A   B   C   D

Researchers→Academic Intermediaries→Research Brokers→Policy Makers

When an item of social science knowledge appears at point A, it is not likely to be in a form that can be directly used at point D, or even

C—even though the research may have been funded by the government itself. In the first place, it may be quite unintelligible to any lay person, written more in algebra than English, full of gammas and deltas and multiple correlations and regression analyses that are explained in forbidding methodological appendices. In the second place, the new research finding probably does not stand alone; it gains meaning only if brought together and interpreted in relation to other bits and pieces of social science data. Finally, it is likely to be inaccessible, published in an obscure journal or simply mimeographed and distributed at conferences, or, in the case of government-funded research, reported to the funding agency but not to legislative committees or other executive agencies to whom it may be pertinent.

The first essential link, then, in the chain of communication is between researchers and academic intermediaries. The latter are men or women within a discipline who have a flair for interpreting, in nontechnical or at least semitechnical language, the technical findings of their colleagues, and who make it their business to do so. They do original research as well, probably, but the findings of their own direct investigations form a small part of the information they assemble and present to the world at large. Their specialty is marketing, not production—and there is need to specialize. Most researchers do well not to try to be their own interpreters and marketers; they do those tasks badly and, when they attempt them, they waste time that could be better spent on more research. By the same token, social scientists with a flair for public relations can best serve their discipline by being the synthesizers and popularizers of its findings—even though they may excite the envy, and even sometimes the scorn, of their colleagues by doing so.

The type comes immediately to mind. They move easily between the academic world and public life. They may have been policy makers themselves, like Wilbur Cohen or George Shultz, or research brokers at the highest level, like Walter Heller or Arthur Okun or Daniel Patrick Moynihan. On leaving public office, they retain contacts with associates who remain in office as policy advisers. They are academicians who are sought out by policy makers when they want the best advice from the social science world—not necessarily because they know more but because they can explain it better. They testify before congressional committees; they serve on presidential task forces; they write less for scholarly journals than for the *New Republic*, the *New York Times*, the *Washington Post*, or even the *Wall Street Journal*. In short, through the media, through hearings and conferences and appearances before many kinds of audiences, and through nontechnical books and articles, they get the findings of social science research into the public domain.

WHERE TRANSMISSION BREAKS DOWN

After the research findings are in the public domain, it is up to research brokers (point C) to find, prepare, and present them for the use of policy makers. While the transmission of social knowledge from A to D (researchers to policy makers), can break down at any point C is invariably the crucial point. Not only is C the most likely breaking point—research brokerage is often missing altogether, badly organized, or poorly staffed—but it is also the point of leverage for getting repairs made when the system breaks down at any other point. Improvements in the performance of A, B, and even D depend upon the initiative and effectiveness of C. Specifically, if A and B are to function better in relation to the government, it will be because of the resources and leadership that flow through C. And if D is to become more sensitive to the work of A and B, the key is likely to be the education that the policy maker receives from the staff associates who function as research brokers.

Point C can be bypassed in the flow of information on occasion, just as can B. As the research broker can learn directly from the researcher without the need for an academic intermediary—to the extent he or she has the time, competence, and staff assistance—so can an academic intermediary communicate directly with a policy maker. But such direct contact, while effective now and then, is rarely satisfactory as a continuing arrangement. Even when policy makers meet with consultants or hear witnesses from the academic community, they ordinarily find it necessary to delegate to a staff assistant the job of maintaining continuous liaison with those advisers in order to study, review, and analyze for policy-making purposes what they have to say.

THE ORGANIZATION OF RESEARCH BROKERAGE

Of foremost concern, then, are the deficiencies in the organization of the research brokerage function throughout the government. The structural variety is great—all the way from ideal to nonexistent. A brief tour of various government offices will illustrate the diversity, both in structure and effectiveness.

Brokerage Models

In the Executive Office of the President is the model for all aspiring research brokers—the Council of Economic Advisers, created by the Employment Act of 1946. The council consists of three members (usually academic economists, normally drawn from the ranks of the academic intermediaries) with substantial staff assistance, designated by law to sit at the elbow of the nation's top policy maker to bring the best of economic knowledge to bear upon policy decisions. And the President is not permitted to ignore them—not totally, anyway, being required by law to submit to the Congress an annual economic report that they draft for him. So at least once a year, the President must read, consider, and ultimately sign their presentation of facts, analyses, interpretations, and proposals.

The enviable status of the Council of Economic Advisors serves only to emphasize the absence of comparable organizations serving other social sciences. Council members have been known to argue that all of social policy is subsumed under the heading of economic policy—just as before 1946 the Bureau of the Budget had been known to contend that economic policy itself is just one aspect of budget policy. But the sociologists, at least, do not agree. Twice their proposal for a Council of Social Advisers in the Executive Office has passed the Senate. To place a Council of Social Advisors beside the Council of Economic Advisors, however, would not solve the whole problem of imbalance. Various task forces and advisory groups, begrudging the special access to the Oval Office of economists, have pleaded for the creation of councils at the presidential level to concern themselves with education, manpower, health, population, urban growth, and various other policy issues. One such plea succeeded: a Council on Environmental Quality was thrust as an unwelcome new member into the Executive Office family. Otherwise, the function of research brokerage is not organized formally at the presidential level.

In the executive departments, the situation is very uneven. Most of the older departments dealing with social or economic policy have research bureaus—the Department of Labor's Bureau of Labor Statistics, the Department of Agriculture's Economic Research Service, the Department of Commerce's Bureau of Economic Analysis and Bureau of the Census, to name a few. Sometimes, as in the case of the Bureau of Labor Statistics, the research bureau was the initial activity around which the department was later built. But these bureaus are some distance removed from the department head. So, at the secretary's level there is, in most cases, an individual, usually an assistant secretary, who with a small staff serves as a link between the department's research organizations and its policy makers—and participates, ordinarily, in the policy-making process: assistant secretary for policy development and research is one such title; economic adviser to the secretary is another; other variations express the same responsibilities. This structure may be replicated in the operating bureaus, in which assistant bureau chiefs or their equivalants may be designated for policy planning and research, and it can extend down to division and unit level, too, although at some point it ceases to be a full-time job and may become simply one duty among many.

On the face of it, such a structure is well suited for the purpose. If social policy making is thought of as a collective process—even though ultimately the policy decision may be made by a single responsible individual—then the research broker is the participant who is responsible for serving as the conduit for the flow of social science information into the policy-making process. If the policy decision is to be made at the departmental level, for example, the department head or a representative will listen to many points of view—not necessarily all at once but in various combinations at different stages of the policy development: the general counsel will advise whether the proposed course of action would or would not get the department into legal difficulties; the line operators will discuss operational feasibility, the additional resources they may need, and how to design and present the policy so as to make it most acceptable to the agency's clientele, or even its own employees; the administrative assistant secretary will talk of budget and personnel requirements and organizational implications; the congressional relations officer will estimate congressional reaction, and make suggestions as to how to counter any adverse response; someone on the secretary's staff (in addition to the congressional liaison officer and, of course, the secretary) will be sensitive to White House views and political repercussions; the information officer will anticipate media reaction, propose means of gaining favorable publicity, and offer ideas for disseminating the policy decision; and someone—and that someone is by definition the research broker—will discuss the proposed policy in terms of what is known in the social sciences about the nature of the problem and the efficacy of alternative approaches that may be available for solving or ameliorating it.

An example of a highly institutionalized research brokerage function is the director of agricultural economics in the Department of Agriculture. The director, aided by a small group of staff economists, is the research broker, with assistant secretary rank. The secretary generally chooses the director, but the choice is made from a limited universe;

the secretary knows that to be useful, the director must be a top agricultural economist who has the full confidence and respect of those in the discipline. The director is in the innermost circle in the Department's decision-making process. It is inconceivable that any decision, even a minor one, affecting production and income in any part of the farming or agribusiness world would be taken without the director's full participation; there have been times, at least, when his stature and command of specialized knowledge resources have either made him the final arbiter of particular agricultural policies or at least given him what amounts to a veto power.

Backing up the director of agricultural economics is the Economic Research Service, which not only has a thousand researchers on its own payroll but also has links with a network of researchers in the land-grant colleges. If a question concerns the likely effect on farm production and income of a major change in agricultural price support levels, for example, the Economic Research Service can quickly provide its own estimates, and, if necessary, can also obtain within a few weeks the independent calculations of a dozen experts from as many different institutions.

That every department and bureau administering social or economic programs needs a research broker to serve in a capacity like that of the Department of Agriculture's director of agricultural economics now seems to be fully recognized. A comparison of government organizational charts of 1975 with those of 1965 or 1955 shows the remarkably rapid growth of an institutionalized research brokerage function at the departmental and bureau levels as well as the beginnings of a standard organizational pattern.

Limitations of Research Brokers

This does not mean, of course, that the function is always as well organized as a chart may indicate. The research brokerage staff may be too small to compete effectively for influence against the large and powerful operating elements of the department or bureau. There are the persistent, seemingly endemic problems of staffing (discussed below). And the function is dependent for its influence upon the existence, in the first place, of an orderly policy-making process. If, for example, policy decisions are concentrated more in the White House, as was the developing pattern during the Nixon administration, research brokers at the departmental level may be (perhaps along with everyone else at that level) quite out of communication when decisions are being made.

Nor does the development of research brokerage functions in the existing departments and bureaus mean that the entire range of social policy is covered. Matters that are not currently the concern of any department are not likely to be anticipated by research brokers. When the prospect of default by New York City arose, for example, the White House, the Treasury Department, and other governmental agencies began a frenzied search for information as to what would happen: Who held the bonds? What would be the immediate effect on the bondholders, and the ripple effect upon the rest of the financial community? What was the plight of other cities? And so on. The information could have been at hand—already analyzed and interpreted—if the default of a major city had been accepted as a matter of federal concern and responsibility, and an intelligence system accordingly had been inaugurated. But research brokers are rarely organized effectively to anticipate problems; their resources are absorbed in collecting and analyzing data pertaining to problems already acknowledged.

On Capitol Hill

On Capitol Hill, the extraordinary fragmentation of policy decisions makes the problem of organizing research brokerage extremely difficult. Responsibility for policy development is parceled out in each house among many committees, each with its independent staff, and then among subcommittees, some of which also have their own staffs and a considerable degree of autonomy. These staffs have the responsibility of performing what research brokerage they can manage along with policy analysis and varied political and administrative duties.

The levels of concentration and proficiency they attain in the research brokerage aspect of their work vary enormously, for the organization of these staffs is the responsibility of a multitude of chairmen who have differing outlooks and comprehensions of their needs. Chairmen—and most of them arrive at their positions by virtue of seniority—may see no need to tap the sources of new knowledge, because the old knowledge, acquired many years ago, still seems adequate. Or, while not adverse to having a bright and able research brokerage staff at their disposal, they may lack the initiative or the skill to find the right people for the jobs. Chairmen turn naturally to lawyers and politicians for their immediate assistance, and those aides may not sense the necessity of using social scientists as advisors—or may fear the competition of those unaccustomed breeds. They may feel that the research brokerage function is done well enough for them by sympathetic interest groups, some of which maintain highly competent staffs in Washington for just that purpose. A subcommittee chairman with grand ambitions for the acquisition of social science talent may be denied such staff by a committee chairman unsympathetic to such designs—and to the policies that such might promote.

Moreover, members of Congress have been accustomed to look to the executive branch to do much of their policy development—and research brokerage—for them. Particularly when the party controlling the Congress also occupies the White House, the President as party leader proposes policy, and the Congress gives that policy a close examination and then votes it up or down. Under such circumstances, a major independent capacity in the Congress for policy development has not been seen as necessary. However, the Congress has been in Democratic hands continuously since 1954, while the Presidency has been occupied by a Republican two-thirds of the time. Congress has been energetic in expanding its own capacity to take the initiative in making policy.

Whether or not a research brokerage capacity exists in a particular congressional committee or subcommittee seems almost accidental. In a few cases, when the chairman happens to have the inclination and the talent to recruit and organize an alert and highly motivated staff, it does have the capacity to reach out into the research community, establish intimate relations with the academic intermediaries, and interpret and apply social science knowledge in the policy-making process. But any careful appraisal would surely show that the well-served policy-making committees are outnumbered by those not so fortunate. Junior legislators who do not have prerogatives as chairmen of committees and subcommittees must rely on their personal staffs for research brokerage. While individual legislative assistants are often surprisingly effective in that capacity, the resources available to rank-and-file senators and representatives are severely limited.

Despairing of the arduous process of trying to build the necessary brokerage capacity on Capitol Hill committee by committee and subcommittee by subcommittee, reformers have looked to the shortcut of creating or strengthening central staffs in the legislative branch, which are available to all committees for research brokerage and related policy analysis and have a universal range of interest and political neutrality. Thus, the Legislative Reference Service of the Library of Congress has been renamed the Congressional Research Service and given an elevated status and expanded staff. Congress has created the Office of Technology Assessment (centered upon the "hard" sciences but with authorization for social policy analysis as well). The Congressional Budget Office has been established as a central analytical capability serving the financial committees of both houses. The General Accounting Office has undergone revolutionary changes, becoming a program evaluator as well as auditor.

All these help, but they are not the whole answer, because the efficiency of the transmission of social knowledge from the research broker to the policy maker—from point C to point D on the diagram above—varies inversely with the distance. A staff that "belongs" to a committee or subcommittee chairman is likely to be utilized. A staff that belongs to someone else and gets supervision and direction from some distant personage, like the Librarian of Congress or the Comptroller General or from a bipartisan supervisory committee, as in the case of the Office of Technology Assessment or the Congressional Budget Office, is not likely to be fully trusted or freely used.

Another reason for this reluctance is related to the neutrality of these bodies: the usefulness on Capitol Hill of neutral policy advice (if that is not a contradiction in terms) is limited. The Congress, after all, contains no neutrals—quite the opposite. Its members make up two highly competitive political forces, subdivided further into contending factions. Each member arrives in Congress with a party and sometimes a factional affiliation as well as a body of policy convictions already established, which he or she may have presented explicitly to the voters for their mandate. As partisans, and perhaps vigorous ones, what the members want is not neutral but partisan advice. They want policy advisers who will obtain from the social science research world the findings that will support their views, or refute the opposition's views. This does not mean that members are intellectually corrupt, only that they recognize that the legislative process has more of the character of an adversary proceeding than of an objective, analytical, scientific undertaking. Perhaps more important, they are realistic in their comprehension of social science. They know that evidence is rarely conclusive and that usually data can be assembled to support any of several points of view in a policy dispute. They want their policy adviser to warn them if their case is totally unsound, and hence politically vulnerable, but short of that to put together the best possible body of data to support the case they have. Even when they are uncommitted and open-minded, they want a policy adviser who is sensitive to their peculiar political needs and ambitions and who will accordingly come up with policy recommendations that will advance both the public's good and their own or their party's or faction's political welfare. This intimate, personalized service can hardly be provided by central and neutral research brokerage organizations.

Centrally located instrumentalities that would be partisan in outlook could be conceived to serve the Congress's majority and minority parties, but since the party organizations have no institutionalized policy-making apparatus of any consequence, there is nothing to which research brokerage can be attached.

So, in the end, it is the decentralized research brokerage structures on Capitol Hill, serving individual committee and subcommittee chairmen and individual members, that need to be strengthened. Indeed, they have been; over the past 20 years, improvement in the capacity of congressional staffs has been little short of spectacular, although the situation is still uneven and will continue to be. The only road to a quick improvement that anyone has been able to think of is to authorize a significant increase in the numbers of staff aides who can be hired. This would produce a greater number of competent staff advisers, assuredly, but whether it would improve the proportion of competent ones, as distinct from party hacks and hometown friends and supporters, is questionable. Committees, subcommittees, and individual members who are already well staffed would be able to improve their staffs even more, but those who do not desire better help, or do not know how to find it, or are not willing to make the effort, would not necessarily be any better served. Capitol Hill would swarm with more staffers of all degrees of competence but the results would still be uneven. And the mere proliferation of staff might tend in itself to make even the most efficient of congressional staff units somewhat less so.

PROBLEMS OF STAFFING AND MANAGEMENT

Research brokerage organizations tend to be unstable. In the legislative branch, committee and subcommittee chairmanships change constantly, with major upheavals possible at the beginning of each Congress; and staff members are wholly dependent on their chairman. In the executive branch, many of the organizations are relatively new and struggling for recognition and influence. Since ambitious people do not seek permanent careers in unstable and insecure surroundings, an almost universal shortcoming of research brokerage organizations is the transient nature of their staffs. They are way stations for persons en route to somewhere else.

The people at point C, the research brokers, are in large measure those on temporary assignment from careers in either academia or the world of policy. On one hand, academicians may want to take a brief fling at public service; from the standpoint of the policy maker, putting a bona fide academician on the staff is a good way to establish effective liaison with the academic community. However, staff members who are also tenured professors can take only limited leave and then must return to reclaim their posts. Those who do not yet have tenure nonetheless plan to return to, or enter upon, their long-run careers of research and teaching. A stint of public service is a worthwhile experience and looks good on a vita, but if they stay with the government too long, they may miss a rung or two on the climb up the ladder of recognition and promotion in the academic world in which their future lies. As research brokers, they keep on the lookout for appropriate posts with more security in the academic world, and when one becomes available, they are likely to seize it.

On the other hand, the research brokerage positions in executive agencies may be occupied by career government employees whose interests lie in program operations and whose aspirations are in administration. Jobs as research brokers need to be filled, and career administrators are willing to accept them as temporary assignments, pending an opportunity to get back into a regular administrative post. Their basic interest is not research, and often they do not devote themselves to mastering what is going on in the research world or learning to interpret it to policy makers. Many find themselves out of sympathy with the ways of academia, irritated by the unintelligibility or seeming irrelevance of much of the research community's work.

In the legislative branch, no corps of career public servants even exists as a ready source of talent for willing chairmen organizing policy development staffs. If a new chairman does not find the previous chairman's staff suitable or (if the predecessor moved on to another chairmanship and took the key staff members) the new chairman has to find some other source of recruits, which is likely to consist of people who happen to be between jobs. Many are young baccalaureates headed for graduate or law school, or law school graduates pausing in Washington on their way back home to set up practice. Accordingly, Capitol Hill staff members tend to be young and inexperienced, and the older ones are all too often those who, facing the necessities of moving from one chairman to another and bridging the many ideological gaps among them, have become cautious to the point of not being effective policy developers at all.

Dynamics of Brokerage

In either branch of the government, if the research brokers come to the job from the academic community, their greatest difficulty is likely to be adjustment to the hurly-burly pace of public affairs. As conscientious social scientists, they may be, when asked for guidance by busy policy makers, not quite sure enough, or not quite quick enough, or not politically wise and sensitive. The policy makers may lose patience: Why does every judgment that comes from the research community have to be qualified? Why does every question need more study? Why do researchers never seem to understand the political necessity for sharp and unequivocal policy positions?

Consider, for instance, what happened when the staff advisers of the Bureau of the Budget to Lyndon Johnson proposed to initiate "community action" as a research experiment rather than as a full-fledged program when the antipoverty effort began. If community action was not a good idea, it should not be tried at all, reasoned the politicians, and if it was a good idea, the more community action agencies that could be created, the better. The research brokers, who had made a quick study of foundation-sponsored experiments in various places, could not be categorical either way, so the political advisers in the White House made the decision, and the go-slow approach that appealed to the research community was rejected. The same thing happened with the model cities program, which was launched in 150 communities instead of in 10 or 20, as the academic authors of the idea had proposed.

Under this kind of pressure, research brokers aspiring for acceptance may find themselves getting into a tell-them-what-they-want-to-hear mood. Since research data rarely support just one side of a case, brokers can readily search out and present with special emphasis the information that reinforces what the policy makers want to do. Research brokers who are essentially administrators may have special long-run interests in pleasing their superiors and less concern than academics about losing face in the research community. The policy maker may never be warned forthrightly that a pending decision flies in the face of the preponderance of social science knowledge. If research brokers do not speak up when the occasion requires, they may preserve the cordiality of their relations with superiors and colleagues, but at the expense of serving the ultimate interests of both policy makers and the research brokerage function.

The amount of resistance that research brokers encounter in presenting unwanted information is likely to increase during the life cycle of a policy idea. If research brokers can bring their findings, analyses, and ideas to bear at the earliest stage of policy development—before the policy makers have become publicly committed to a course of action—they can probably be forceful without risk to their relationship. At an early stage in policy development, they need not worry about telling their principals merely what they want to hear, because they will not yet know what they want. In this situation, research brokers have the opportunity to initiate the policy development and steer its course. At this time, too, they can best make use of outside allies—task forces, study commissions—that can review research findings and analyses and help to arrive at policy recommendations with the added weight of their approval.

Once policy makers have declared a public position, the whole situation is changed. Then, research brokers may find themselves unable to use social science information to influence the main current of events. They must swallow their misgivings, if they have any, and maintain a public silence. But—and this can be most important—they may be able to build a research component into the policy itself. Particularly in the case of new programs or major alterations in old programs, they can press for evaluation studies to monitor the results of the policy departure.

If the evaluation results are negative, the research brokers may be put to their severest test. The files of federal agencies contain not a few evaluation studies that have been suppressed because they brought forth the "wrong" findings. Suppression is more difficult since passage of the Freedom of Information Act (and even before the Act, the results of such studies had a way of leaking), but suppression still occurs. And then research brokers are caught hopelessly in the middle: if they are party to concealment or even to delay in the release of data, they jeopardize their standing with the research community. If they insist on publication of the findings, they risk their standing with their superiors in the agency.

In summary, then, the pitfalls of research brokerage are uncertainty in giving advice when policy makers look for certainty; support for a favored policy course when the facts call for caution; negative findings when policy makers seek support (or vice versa). Threading a course among these hazards is never easy, and it is difficult even to lay out general rules of conduct. The simple guide, "Be honest," is a start, but that leaves open the question of how vigorously one presses an honest case. Much depends on the personal attributes of research brokers themselves—tact, confidence, sense of timing, verbal facility, and skill in building alliances within the policy-making community. These can, to a degree, be improved through experience, but the short-term assignments that characterize research brokerage preclude putting much experience to use. By the time research brokers are at home in their surroundings and ready to perform at maximum proficiency, they are likely to be gone.

And much, of course, is out of their hands. The personal attributes of the policy maker or the policy-making group may be determining: if they are headstrong or anti-intellectual, or if they feel compelled by political circumstance to go their way despite the counseling of social science, there is not much that can be done about it. A democratic political process is bound to advance some policy makers who do not have the interest, the patience, or the administrative competence to make effective use of social science knowledge. Presumably, in time, as social science gains more authority in society at large, the willingness and ability of policy makers to make use of research findings will become a factor in their own election or appointment. A trend in that direction seems evident already, if one merely observes the remarkable increase in the number of Ph.Ds in the cabinet and even in the Congress in recent years. Economic advice to Presidents and members of Congress, for instance, used to come primarily from businessmen, bankers, and stockbrokers. Now, the academic economists have most of the policy influence, and the shift is not an accidental one. Academicians are the ones who have roots in, and presumably keep in closest touch with, the research community where knowledge is being generated; policy makers who are cut off from it feel uneasy.

Making use of advisors from the academic world still leaves policy makers most of the room for maneuvering that they may want. Using economics again as the case in point, conservative Presidents find it possible to find conservative academics to advise them on the interpretation of research findings, and liberal congressional committees are able to find liberal economists to provide them with the opposite interpretation. Perhaps there is no such thing as an ideologically neutral economist, or perhaps nobody in partisan Washington wants to have one around. That these circumstances sometimes lead to an attitude, on the part of the policy maker, of "tell me what I want to hear or I'll find somebody who will" can hardly be denied. But even at worst, proposals considered by the policy maker will have been analyzed by competent, if ideologically biased, brokers in light of evidence produced by the research community. That, after all, is all that the research community can ask. Policy advice is the social scientists' prerogative, not policy decisions. It is the right of a democratic people to make mistakes, even to make them knowingly, and when policy makers are under great public pressure to follow a misguided course of action, they can be expected, most of the time, to do so.

Social scientists must learn to accept this and learn how to put it to advantage. For societies as well as individuals, trial and error is a basic way of learning. When risky policies and programs are about to be launched is the time to press for systematic observation and analysis in order to make them the richest possible societal learning experience. Congress has been remarkably receptive to requests for funds for evaluation; no social programs were ever more generously endowed with moneys for that purpose than those begun under Johnson's "Great Society." The current widespread feeling that those ventures failed has, if anything, strengthened the position of those who want more and better evaluations.

Indeed, policies often have to be launched in a research vacuum, because not until something happens can the consequences of that happening be discerned. For example, the data that Herbert Gans developed on the consequences of breaking up an ethnic community in Boston through the urban renewal program could not have been assembled until the breakup occurred. Perhaps the multiple pathologies of high-rise public housing projects could have been fore-seen, but they could hardly have been described to policy makers in convincing detail before the buildings had been built and occupied. Moreover, funds for policy-related research are not usually available in quantity for policies that are only potential, and the interest of re-searchers is attracted more by the actual and the imminent than by the speculative. When the government becomes interested in a neglected field of policy, it may do so suddenly (as in the case of the antipoverty program) and ask for immediate answers that the research community does not have. Then those who counsel delay while the research is being done may be overwhelmed by the political forces that press for immediate action. So evaluation, while second best to prior analysis, is often the only type of policy research that time allows.

The research community would be caught less often unprepared, of course, if government research programs were deliberately expanded to encompass as much as possible of the range of potential, as distinct from actual, policy. The National Science Foundation is one agency not limited to existing policies in its mission, but it is a research funding agency rather than a research broker. Departments, bureaus, and congressional committees need research brokers to broaden their scope; research on everything that is happening and might happen to cities, for instance, should concern the Department of Housing and Urban Development. However, two factors militate against such broader scope. One is the pressure of demand upon limited resources: when the choice is between gathering data on current policy alterna-tives or on alternatives that might become feasible or necessary in the future, the resources inevitably are devoted to the former. The second is the tendency of policy makers to look upon research relating to possible new policies as subversive of the existing policies to which they are politically committed. Policy makers simply have to become more tolerant of futurism; they need to set aside resources for the future minded to use and insulate these thinkers from the pressure of current issues. Policy makers must come to realize that the future is often closer than they think—as the New York City fiscal crisis demonstrated. Changing the outlook of policy makers, however, is always a large order, and, once more, the research broker is the crucial link in the chain. If policy makers are to be educated to these facts of life, the research brokers will have to do it.

THE REVERSE FLOW OF LEADERSHIP AND FUNDS

Another aspect of the research broker's role will be touched on only briefly here: the broker's responsibility for providing leadership, guidance, and resources to enable the research community to serve the needs of social policy. This can be shown as a reverse flow along a communication channel like the one diagrammed at the beginning of this paper:

A	B	C	D
	Research	Information	
Researchers←Administrators←(Research) Brokers←Policy Makers			

This channel carries not just information but also money. A different term is used for B; this time he or she is the research administrator, who may or may not be the same person as the academic intermediary we met earlier. But C is usually the same: one element of the department or bureau deals with the academic community both in stimulating and funding research and in interpreting findings.

Like the A-B-C-D flow of information, the D-C-B-A flow can also break down at any point. But again, it is instructive to look especially at point C, for if the private research community fails the government, it is once more through the leverage of the institutionalized brokerage function that improvement can be attained. Research capability is so scattered—necessarily so—that it is incumbent on the research broker to make the research community work for the government through care in the allocation of research funds and guidance in their use.

The same weaknesses that impair the effectiveness of research brokers in interpreting social science information to policy makers hinder them in their role as guides and stimulators of research. Again, the tell-them-what-they-want-to-hear attitude may prevail, but this time "them" is the research community. Let the researchers, in other words, do what they want to do. So the researchers initiate projects, which are evaluated by their peers in the research community, and funds are awarded accordingly. The relevance to actual policy making—that is, the subsequent flow of useful data from A to D—may be neglected.

This can hardly be blamed on policy makers. Policy makers as such should not have to contribute to the process of research design or to help appraise the qualifications of research institutions or even to give much concentrated thought to the identification of research needs. These are the elements of research administration, and research brokers should be close enough to the policy-making process to take responsibility for them. If the brokers are not close enough for those tasks, then they are not close enough for any purpose. In that situation, there is, in effect, no research brokerage function and one should be established.

When policy makers delegate the job of research administration to research brokers with a minimum of supervision and control, the easy course for the latter, in turn, is to delegate initiative and control to researchers. Such an arrangement is at times formalized in the establishment of government-supported research institutes that are left free, or nearly so, to design their own programs and choose their own topics. Even a government research bureau may be left essentially autonomous to frame its own research agenda.

It requires the assertion of authority by research brokers, representing the interests of policy makers, to ensure that research findings are of maximum utility to policy makers. To put it another way, the more that federal officials participate in the determination of the research agenda, the more applied research will be emphasized, even though basic research may be closer to researchers' interests. This does not rule out government encouragement of basic social science research altogether, but it is incumbent upon agencies that appropriate research funds to use at least the major share of those funds for purposes as practical as can be conceived. The research does not have to be for immediate application. As suggested earlier, studies leading to the initiation of a new program or policy 3 or 5 years hence may be of highest priority, but this is still within the definition of practical, applied research, and it still needs to be designed with a high degree of government participation. In any case, research for immediate problems is likely to advance long-range and basic research as well; social scientists can well learn from their counterparts in the physical sciences that the successful application of research to current, specific, and urgent policy problems has a way of endearing the whole idea of research to policy makers, winning them over to the support of all types of studies.

RESEARCH BROKERAGE—A NEW DISCIPLINE?

All of the weaknesses in the performance of the research brokerage function discussed above appear as inevitable reflections of its present state of underdevelopment, and they will gradually be overcome as research brokerage becomes more clearly recognized and solidly established as one of the necessary and continuing staff functions serving the policy maker—as essential to effective administration as, say, budgeting, personnel administration, or the procurement and distribution of supplies. Universal acceptance would bring with it stability and continuity, which in turn would make possible the development of a new, self-conscious breed of research brokers—men and women who would point their careers toward the development of that function, who would look upon research brokerage as a goal rather than a way station, who would stay in the activity long enough to do it well, and who would devote themselves to developing and standardizing the doctrines that need to govern its performance. If career training could be devised, too, the makings of an identifiable discipline, profession, or subdiscipline would be at hand.

The new schools of public policy that have sprung up in so many universities appear to be striving, more or less consciously, to create just such a discipline. They are not in business to professionalize policy making as such; some of their graduates may become policy makers, but that will be accidental. They can hardly hope, soon if ever, to compete with the law schools or even the departments of economics in turning out cabinet members, presidential advisers, and members of Congress. But they can professionalize the link between policy making and social knowledge by turning out a corps of graduates with a sophisticated understanding of the importance of maintaining a flow of facts and interpretation from the world of research to the world of action and a flow of leadership and support back again—and who will, one may hope, develop the competence to live happily in the borderland between both worlds, communicating equally well with the denizens of each.

The Use of
Social Research
in the Courts

SHARON M. COLLINS

> To secure social advance . . . we must regard . . . sociology and social legislation as a field for discovery and invention (Justice Louis Brandeis, *The Brandeis Guide to the Modern World*, 1941).

OVERVIEW

In the abstract, the attempts of social sciences and the law to understand, explain, and order human behavior appear to have much in common. In practice, however, they differ fundamentally. Since the function of the social sciences is observation and evaluation, their nature is passive and their focus is on a macroscale. In essence, the social sciences provide theoretical scaffolds, supporting the accumulation of knowledge about human behavior in order to analyze its effect on society. In contrast, legal inquiry focuses on solving the specific problems presented by each particular case. Compared to the social sciences, its role is dynamic, its goal more concrete and immediate, and its research much narrower in scope. Thus, whereas social research analyzes collections of data and generalizes, legal research evaluates and orders individual, finite situations.

In the past century, these differences in method, precision, and perspective have impeded sociolegal cooperation rather than formed

Sharon M. Collins is a student at Cornell University Law School. This paper was prepared for the Study Project on Social Research and Development in 1975.

the bases of a complementary relationship. Skeptical of the competence of social science research and unsure of their own evaluative abilities, most lawyers have been reluctant to tap the resources of the social sciences. Even when individual attorneys have chosen to support their arguments with social science research, the evidence still faced another, frequently more stringent, test: acceptance by the judge. The decision of the judge regarding admission of evidence depends on the determination of both its logical and—particularly important with respect to social science data—legal relevance. Not only must the evidence tend to prove a consequential fact (Rule 401, Federal Rules of Evidence), but its probative value must outweigh any countervailing policy considerations (Rule 403, Federal Rules of Evidence).

Regarding admission of social science evidence, the four variables of logical relevance, quantifiability, lack of value judgments, and concern for the individual bear strongly on its credibility and are balanced frequently against the dangers of unfair prejudice, confusing the issues, misleading the jury, delay, or needlessly presenting cumulative evidence (Robbins 1975, p. 493). In considering such evidence, quantifiability is usually equated with accuracy. Similarly, implicit value judgments automatically evoke suspicion. But on the whole, concern for the individual dominates. This concern is the major dividing force between social scientists and lawyers: while social scientists may criticize the narrow scope of law, lawyers, with matching intensity, mistrust the generalities of social science. In short, although recognizing that aggregate data are the very lifeblood of social science projections, most lawyers feel that full-scale use of the social science approach in the judicial system would be disastrous. Justice cannot be rendered in generalities; each case must be decided on its facts. Moreover, many judges feel that "[i]t is not within [the] . . . competence [of the courts] to confirm or deny claims of social scientists as to the status of an individual in the community" (*Beauharnais v. Illinois*, 343 U.S. 250, 263 [1952]).

Despite the mutual skepticism between social scientists and lawyers, the existence of a common goal implies a vast potential for social benefit. Ideally, in a system of sociolegal cooperation, law would become the medium for the transition of social research from a passive to an active role—for the transformation of theoretical solutions into social actions (Lochner 1973). In turn, the results of enlightened social science research could facilitate judicial interpretation in accordance with current social needs, establish relevant factual evidence, and serve as a "surrogate precedent," supporting judicial treatment of publicly sensitive issues. Law would thus enhance the practical aspects of the social sciences, and, conversely, social science data would enrich legal analysis with evidence otherwise beyond its scope.

However, the present relationship between social research and the law is not yet stable, and fruitful social science-legal cooperation is only in its beginning stages. Its development has had a capricious, sporadic evolution. As a result, even though the use of social research in the courts has intensified, particularly in the past decade, sociolegal cooperation is nowhere near the realization of its full potential.

This paper deals with the present relationship of social science to the law, and specifically the extent to which the courts are using social science research. Ranked according to use, the four types of social research and development most commonly incorporated into legal cases are: (1) expert testimony, (2) results of existing studies, (3) public opinion polls, and (4) results of studies conducted specifically for the case at hand. Social research used within the legal system is primarily either evaluative or predictive. Of the two, more weight has been accorded to the former.

Legal input from particular social science disciplines ranges widely. At one extreme, economics is used relatively intensively; at the other, anthropology is seldom used. Psychological and sociological research, although frequently relevant, is more controversial, and thus engenders a higher degree of skepticism; its use lies between the two extremes.

Of all social science research, economic evidence regarding labor, antitrust, trade regulations, trademarks, licensing, taxation, and corporations has been used most extensively by the courts. Partial explanation for its frequent use is that economics, the most quantitative of the social sciences, ostensibly has fewer of the flaws that lawyers perceive as inherent in social science. Considered relatively precise, economics appears to leave little room for value judgments. Public opinion surveys also rank among the most widely used and universally accepted social science evidence. At present, the use of surveys dealing with government regulations and trademarks is fairly well established; more recently developed surveys dealing with the determination of community bias and the effects of segregation do not yet stand on firm legal ground. In contrast, statistical analysis, relying to a large extent on probability theory, has failed to earn the respect of the majority of those in the legal profession. Statistics have been particularly misused in criminal cases dealing with the establishment of guilt, although they have been a valuable tool in dealing with jury bias, jury size, and bail and pretrial detention.

Psychological, sociological, and socioeconomic evidence, applicable to a wider spectrum of cases, meets with a much more varied reception. Psychological evidence has been used in determining mental competency, predicting criminal dangerousness, and defining criminal responsibility. Sociological evidence has been introduced primarily in cases concerning segregation and education, although in recent years it has been extended to cases dealing with employment discrimination and surveillance. Although the relevance of sociologically based research to societal conditions can no longer be denied, lawyers remain skeptical of its value judgments, imprecisions, and distortions. Thus, socioeconomic evidence is used less frequently; herein it is cited in reference to public school financing. Anthropology, rarely used, is mentioned solely in reference to an antimiscegenation case.

SOCIAL SCIENCE APPLICATIONS

ECONOMIC RESEARCH

The judicial system since its inception has relied almost exclusively on judicial precedent in formulating its decisions. Only since the turn of the century has social science evidence provided a supplementary data base. Although *Muller v. Oregon* (208 U.S. 412 [1908]), with the introduction of the "Brandeis brief," stands as the landmark case for the use of economic data in support of a legal argument, the first use of social science data actually occurred 3 years earlier in *Lochner v. New York* (198 U.S. 45 [1905]).

Typical of the early labor cases, *Lochner* involved a conflict between the exercise of the state's police power to legislate labor regulations protecting the health, safety, morals, and general welfare of its citizens and the possible infringement on the individual's right to contract. The question was, how far did state police power extend before it unreasonably restricted individual liberty? In *Lochner*, the Supreme Court invalidated New York's labor law limiting the workday of bakers to 10 hours (N.Y. laws of 1897, art. 8, c. 415, §110), holding that, since the trade was not dangerous in any degree to the health of the employees, there was "no reasonable foundation to justify regarding it as a health law" (198 U.S. at 58, 64). Thus, the real purpose of the legislation was simply to regulate the hours of labor, and as such was an unconstitutional limitation on the right to contract. The inference of *Lochner* was that the state's police power to regulate conditions of labor could be invoked only in the event of gross occupational hazards; without such danger, state interference would infringe on individual liberties. In the words of the Court, "[s]ome occupations are more healthy than others, but . . . [t]here must be more than the mere fact of the possible existence of some small amount of unhealthiness to warrant legislative interference with liberty" (198 U.S. 45 at 59).

Critical to shifting the balance in the *Lochner* decision was evidence presented regarding the dangers inherent to the baking industry. Whereas the state based its argument solely on the propriety of the exercise of police power, the employer's brief asserted "there was no danger to the employee in a first-class bakery" and supported its argument with a set of tables comparing the mortality rates and the health dangers of specific trades (198 U.S. 45 at 49 and accompanying notes). Since the data were slanted to depict ideal working conditions in bakeries, and actual conditions were not well publicized, the employer's brief carried considerable weight. Had a "reasonable-man" standard been applied as Justice Oliver Wendell Holmes insisted in his dissent (198 U.S. 45 at 75), the Court would have reached a totally opposite decision. Instead, biased research presented in the employer's brief circumvented the traditional standard and succeeded in influencing a majority of the Court. Social research and development was off to a roaring start—on the wrong foot.

The Brandeis Precedent

Three years later, Louis Brandeis's introduction of the first formal brief relying heavily on social science research in *Muller v. Oregon* (208 U.S. 412 [1908]) marked a new era in jurisprudence. *Muller* upheld the constitutionality of an Oregon statute limiting the workday of women employed in laundries to 10 hours (1903 Or. Sess. Laws, §1). In arguing for fair labor standards, Brandeis's strategy was to persuade the "business community that labor welfare measures were not only compatible with, but actually beneficial to business interests" (Cohen 1943, p. 388). Thus his first briefs were not sociological in content, but economic, drawing on surveys, government statistics, and factory reports, designed to convince the Court of the statute's benefit to society and lack of constitutional harm.

Working with social worker Josephine Goldberg, Brandeis argued that not only were long work hours detrimental to the women's health, but that in the long run, shorter hours resulted in general economic benefits for the entire community (Cohen 1943, p. 388). The opinion of the Court mentioned the supralegal material in the Brandeis brief and, in apparent deference to the Holmes dissent in *Lochner*, acknowledged that although the sources were neither technical authorities nor discussions of the relevant constitutional questions, they were indicative of wide-spread belief. The Court noted that even though constitutional questions "are not settled by a consensus of present public opinion, . . . when a question of fact is debated and the extent to which a special constitutional limitation goes is affected by the truth in respect to that fact, a widespread and long continued belief concerning it is worthy of consideration" (208 U.S. 412 at 420, 421 [1908]) (Ziskind 1939, p. 607).

The Court's acceptance of the Brandeis brief in *Muller v. Oregon* officially opened the door to the use of a wide range of supralegal material. In the following years, numerous cases patterned after *Muller* argued by Brandeis and later by Felix Frankfurter used the Brandeis brief in advocating the merits of social legislation as a boon to efficiency, commercial prosperity, and social welfare. *Hawley v. Walker* (232 U.S. 718 [1914]) upheld an Ohio statute that regulated the work hours of women in factories. *Miller v. Wilson* (263 U.S. 373 [1914]) and *Bosley v. McLaughlin* (236 U.S. 385 [1914]) upheld the validity of a California statute limiting a woman's workday to 8 hours. And in *People v. Schweinler Press* (214 N.Y. 395, 108 N.E. 639 [1915]) the Brandeis-Goldberg brief contained an 80-page analysis of the effect on business of outlawing night work for women (Cohen 1943, p. 380). Three years later, following Brandeis's appointment to the Supreme Court, Frankfurter carried on the tradition. With the aid of economic research, he successfully argued *Bunting v. Oregon* (243 U.S. 426 [1917]), which upheld the regulation of hours for male factory workers, and *Stettler v. O'Hara* (243 U.S. 629 [1917]), which upheld minimum wage legislation for women.

Within a short period of time, the Brandeis brief had turned an attitude into a technique. In the wake of the Brandeis-Frankfurter success, other lawyers soon began to imitate their method. *Hammer v. Dagenhart* (247 U.S. 251 [1918]), for example, relied on legislative committee reports and economic studies to expose the harm of child labor.

Not all of the social-science-based arguments presented during this period were successful. The Frankfurter brief prepared for *Adkin v. Children's Hospital* (261 U.S. 525 [1923]) contained a 30-page appendix entitled "Industrial Efficiency of Both Employers and Employees Stimulated." Drawn from a thesis of Hobson (1910), the brief argued for a fixed minimum wage for women and proposed that higher wages would stimulate greater industrial efficiency (Cohen 1943, p. 397). It failed, however, to convince the Court. Fourteen years later, the effort to raise women's wages was revived. In *Morehead v. People ex rel. Tipaldo* (298 U.S. 587 [1936]) the brief of the State of New York presented statistical and economic evidence to prove that, since *Adkin* was argued, the number of female breadwinners had substantially increased. The state urged that this fact, coupled with the effects of the Depression, underscored the need for wage regulation. The attempt again failed, as the Court stated that the facts of law had not changed.

Similarly, in another Depression-era case, *Schecter Poultry Corp. v. United States* (295 U.S. 495 [1935]), the government, arguing unsuccessfully for a regulated wage increase, presented evidence of the wage and employment decline, overproduction, cutthroat competition, and reduced purchasing power in the poultry industry. Economic analysis revealed that, in times of economic emergency, the cumulative effect of these conditions was to further depress prices, to induce sale of inferior products, and to initiate a downward spiral in consumption. The government concluded that such practices contributed to a material frustration of interstate commerce, and reversal of the process through federal regulation was critical to economic recovery (295 U.S. 495 at 509-513). The Court did not rely on the economic evidence in its decision; it held that, since grave national crises "do not create or enlarge Constitutional power" (295 U.S. 495 at 528), it would not authorize federal regulation of wages and hours. Again, the evidence of social research and development failed to alter the Court's concept of the law.

Strikes and Boycotts

Just as the first labor-wage decisions were based on the strictly legal arguments of the state's police power, early strike and boycott cases relied solely on the determination of restraint of trade—instead of the deliberate use of economic data.[1] In this situation, *Coronado Coal Company v. United Mine Workers* (268 U.S. 295 [1925]) marked the turning point. Strikes and riots by the United Mine Workers had caused the mine management to change from union to open shop. This move was challenged in court by the unions. In 1922, the Supreme

[1] See, for example, *United States v. Brims*, 272 U.S. 549 (1926) (conspiracy to restrain competition illegal); *Industrial Association of San Francisco v. United States*, 268 U.S. 64 (1925) (closed shop illegal); *United Leather Worker International Union v. Herkert*, 265 U.S. 457 (1924) (strike in restraint of trade); *Duplex Printing Press Co. v. Deering*, 254 U.S. 443 (1921) (secondary boycotts unauthorized by Clayton Act); and *Gompers v. Bucks Stove and Range Co.*, 221 U.S. 418 (1911) (secondary boycott with intent to curtail interest trade of nonunion firms illegal.)

Court decided in favor of the unions, holding the strike to be of a purely local nature (259 U.S. 344 at 413 [1922]). Although the Court acknowledged the union's intent to affect operation of the mines (259 U.S. 344 at 400-403), it did not consider the evidence sufficient to support a finding of conspiracy to restrain interstate commerce (259 U.S. 344 at 408-9). The case was remanded to the district court for further proceedings and reached the Supreme Court again in 1925.

On the second appeal to the Supreme Court, the company took full advantage of the general economic background of the case. Asserting that the purpose of the strike was to halt the production and prevent the interstate shipment of nonunion coal, the company supported its argument with supplementary economic evidence connecting the strike with a scheme for the preserving union organization. The company produced data proving that mines with open shops were not only cheaper to run but also seven times more efficient than union mines. Moreover, it established that 80 percent of the output of the striking mines went into interstate commerce and from that projected the competitive effect on the price of the coal. Finally, the company argued that the general policy of the union was to increase the price of coal in one area in order to protect the union operators elsewhere. The logical inference was that union control hindered competition and adversely influenced the market price of coal (Ziskind 1939, pp. 611, 612; 268 U.S. 295 at 308-10). The company's argument was persuasive. On the basis of the economic data, the Supreme Court overruled portions of its previous decision, stating that the reality of the union's interest in protecting its organization throughout the coal areas of the United States was, in the words of the Court, "too stark to conceal."

The National Labor Relations Board

By the 1930s, the use of the Brandeis brief had definitely infiltrated the judicial system. Although not always successful, the use of supplemental data was considered for the most part relevant, useful, and—to a more variable degree—necessary. For example, in *Lauf v. E.G. Shinner* (303 U.S. 323 [1938]) and *Senn v. Tile Layers Protective Union* (301 U.S. 468 [1937]), the Supreme Court accepted the economic theories proposed and incorporated them into its opinions. In the mid-1930s, the U.S. Division of Economic Research (DER) was created within the National Labor Relations Board (NLRB) for the express purpose of preparing industrial studies and supporting expert testimony by labor economists for use in labor suits. To this end, the first five cases brought by the NLRB were deliberately planned to make use of DER data.

NLRB v. Jones & Laughlin Steel Corp. (301 U.S. 1 [1937]), in which DER economists collaborated with NLRB lawyers in preparing a brief supporting the Wagner Act, is the landmark. Convinced by the economic research, the majority opinion stated that even intrastate activities may fall within federal control when closely and intimately related to interstate commerce (301 U.S. 1 at 37, 38) and held that industrial strikes resulting from an absence of collective bargaining cause a direct and proximate obstruction to the flow of interstate commerce (301 U.S. 1 at 42). In four cases before the Supreme Court immediately following *Jones & Laughlin* (*NLRB v. Freuhauf Trailer Company*, 301 U.S. 49 [1937]; *NLRB v. Friedman-Harry Marks Clothing Co., 301 U.S. 58* [1937]; *Associated Press v. NLRB*, 301 U.S. 103 [1937]; and *Washington, Virginia and Maryland Coach Co. v. NRLB*, 301 U.S. 142 [1937] the NLRB relied heavily upon the economic evidence initially prepared for the *Jones* case.

After these five cases, the NLRB's use of economic data varied considerably. It is plausible that once it became clear that the Supreme Court fully and sympathetically understood the economic issues pertaining to labor relations, the DER saw no need to provide supplementary data (Ziskind 1939, p. 630). And, to a degree, the decisions of the Supreme Court support this hypothesis. *NLRB v. Pennsylvania Greyhound Lines, Inc.* (303 U.S. 261 [1938]) and *NLRB v. Pacific Greyhound Lines, Inc.* (303 U.S. 272 [1938]), which affirmed the power of the NLRB to order the dissolution of a company union, *Santa Cruz Co. v. NLRB* (303 U.S. 453 [1938]) and *Consolidated Edison Co. of N.Y. v. NLRB* (304 U.S. 555 [1939]), which upheld collective bargaining, and *NLRB v. Mackay Radio and Telegraph Co.* (304 U.S. 333 [1938]), which affirmed the power of the NLRB to reinstate workers after an unsuccessful strike, were all argued without any supporting economic data. Whether the same results would have been reached without the alleged sensitizing of the Court, however, is limited to speculation.

Conclusion

The Brandeis brief paved the way for the use of social science data in court decisions. Although it was never intended to displace constitutional standards, the use of social science analysis in early labor cases, beginning with *Muller v. Oregon*, did signify a departure from the traditional, strictly legal, bases for decision. From then on, the courts witnessed the gradual assimilation and expansion of social science evidence. Indeed, by the 1930s, the use of economic data was well on the way toward firm acceptance by the courts. In the late 1930s, however, the Court began to shift from a focus on primarily economic issues to one of individual liberties. Consequently, the relative predominance of economically oriented cases began to fade.

STATISTICAL DATA

The use of statistics and probabilistic evidence in the courtroom directly confronts a profound legal issue: how to cope with uncertainty in a direct and orderly manner. Usually, the basic probabilistic ideas remain unexpressed and serve only as mental guides for judges and juries, but sometimes they are made explicit and cast in mathematical terms. This has occurred most frequently in criminal cases in which probability theory has been offered to establish guilt and statistical determination of bias has been applied to jury representation.

Criminal Law and Probability

Criminal law has served as the forum for the most extensive and intensely debated application of probability theory. The major objection to its use comes from the premise that, by design, probabilistic reasoning serves as the basis for the statistical prediction of a future event, not for deciding whether an alleged past event actually occurred. Critics assert that probability concepts should have no bearing on determining whether a specific event actually occurred. "Either it did or didn't happen—period" (Tribe 1971, p. 1344). Others argue that the factor of uncertainty common to both past and future events justifies the use of probability reasoning. Practical experience has further heated the debate. Ironically, many uses of probability evidence in criminal proceedings have been grossly erroneous. As a result, the use of applied probability in legal proceedings to assess the significance of evidence is highly controversial (Kingston 1966, p. 93).

To illustrate, in the cases of *People v. Risley* (214 N.Y. 75, 108 N.E. 200 [1915]), *State v. Sneed* (76 N.M. 349, 414 P.2d 858 [1966]), *Miller v. State* (240 Ark. 340, 399 S.W.2d 268 [1966]), and *People v. Collins* (68 Cal. 2d 319, 438 P.2d 33, 66 Cal. Rptr. 497 [1968]), expert probability testimony was presented specifically to assess the weight of circumstantial evidence. In each case, the testimony provided grounds for reversal on appeal; all were remanded for retrials with instructions to exclude the probability evidence.

In *People v. Risley*, an attorney was prosecuted for offering in evidence a document that he knew had been fraudulently altered by the insertion of typewritten words. At trial, as the major part of the proof that the instrument was altered by the use of a typewriter in the defendant's law office, the state called a mathematics professor who testified to the mathematical probability that the words inserted in the document were typed on the defendant's typewriter (214 N.Y. 75 at 84, 85). Although the defendant was convicted in the trial court, the New York Court of Appeals held that the "admission of the evidence was error, prejudicial to the interests of the defendant . . . and . . . an attempt to draw a line between assumed fact and reasonable conclusion to an extent never recognized by this court" (214 N.Y. 75 at 87). Its directive was clear. Such calculations, based on speculation, not on actual observation, were to be distinguished from more acceptable types of statistical evidence.

In like manner, the mathematical testimony used in the murder trial of *State v. Sneed* was considered factually insufficient and held inadmissible on appeal. The state's witness, again a professor of mathematics, presented an estimate of probability correlating the appearance of a given surname in telephone books, the probability of the combination of the defendant's physical characteristics appearing throughout the population, and the probability of choosing certain pawnshop numbers within a given time period. The court of appeals held that the probability estimates were miscalculated and lacked sufficient basis and further stated that "mathematical odds are not admissible as evidence to identify a defendant in a criminal proceeding so long as the odds are based on estimates" (76 N.M. 349 at 354, 414 P.2d 858 at 862).

In *Miller v. State*, a burglary conviction was reversed on the grounds that the probability testimony of a chemist who had examined specimens of dirt found on the defendant's clothing near the scene of the crime was unsubstantiated, speculative, and conjectural. In holding the testimony inadmissible, the court indicated that the expert witness had made no tests on which he could reasonably base his probabilities, that he did not base his testimony on studies of such tests made by others, and that he admitted his figures were predicted on estimates and assumptions (240 Ark. at 343, 344). This probability testimony, allegedly lacking adequate foundation, constituted the only ground for reversal (Cullison 1969, p. 517).

The most infamous probability case is that of *People v. Collins* involving the robbery prosecution of a black man and his white wife. In its highly circumstantial case, the state presented testimony of a mathematics professor who attempted to link the defendants statistically to the crime—purely by merit of physical appearance. Without requiring statistical verification, the prosecutor allowed the witness to "assume probability factors for the various characteristics that he deemed to be shared by the guilty couple and all other couples answering to such distinctive characteristics'' (69 Cal. 2d at 325, 438 P.2d at 39, 66 Cal. Rptr. at 502). Then, reasoning that the probability of the joint occurrence of a number of mutually independent events was equal to the product of the individual probabilities that each of the events will occur, the prosecutor calculated that ''there was but one chance in 12 million that any couple possessed the distinctive characteristics of the defendants'' (p. 502). The jurors, ''undoubtedly unduly impressed by the mystique of the mathematical demonstration, but . . . unable to assess the relevancy of its value,'' found the defendants guilty (Cullison 1969, p. 516; 68 Cal. 2d 319 at 332, 438 P.2d 33 at 41, 66 Cal Rptr. 497 at 505).

On appeal, the California Supreme Court reversed, stating:

We deal here with the novel question of whether evidence of mathematical probability has been properly introduced and used by prosecution in a criminal case. While we discern no inherent incompatibility between the disciplines of law and mathematics and intend no general disapproval or disparagement of the latter as an auxiliary in the fact-finding processes of the former, we cannot uphold the technique employed in the instant case . . . [because it] infected the case with fatal error and distorted the jury's traditional role of determining guilt or innocence according to long settled rules. Mathematics, a veritable sorcerer in our computerized society, while assisting the trier of fact in the search for truth must not cast a spell over him. We conclude that on the record before us, the defendant should not have had his guilt determined by the odds and that he is entitled to a new trial (68 Cal. 2d 319 at 320, 438 P.2d at 33).

The use of mathematical probability injected two fundamental prejudicial errors. First, the testimony lacked adequate foundation, and, second, the manner in which it was used distracted the jury from properly weighing the evidence, encouraging reliance upon an irrelevant expert demonstration. This tactic not only placed the jurors and the defense counsel at a disadvantage, but denied the defendant an effective defense (66 Cal. 2d at 327, 438 P.2d at 41).

The *Collins* decision marked a step—albeit by some interpretations a step backward—in the developing relationship between social science research and law. Its significance lies in the fact that the judges considered the statistical sortie seriously enough to comment extensively on the problem of statistical proofs, and to attempt to present the correct form for such mathematical analysis (Finklestein and Fairley 1970, p. 489).

The common thread among these probability cases is the unwillingness of the courts to accept statistical speculation. Courts may accept a statistical interpretation if it is based on existing, precisely measurable data (such as life expectancy and occupational mortality rates), but, particularly in criminal law, they have resisted persuasion by mere statistical interpretations of odds.

Jury Bias

PROPORTIONAL REPRESENTATION   The determination of jury bias pertaining to both population representation and adequacy of jury size represents another aspect of the use of statistics in the legal arena. Used since the 1940s, these analyses have met with limited success—but for a different reason. At issue is neither the statistical integrity of the evidence nor its probative value, but its relative worth in light of stronger constitutional considerations.

Testimony focusing on the alleged local practice of the systematic exclusion of blacks from grand juries and subsequent disproportionate representation relative to the population played a major role in the Supreme Court reversal of a murder conviction in *Hill v. Texas* (316 U.S. 400 [1942]). Hill argued that the exclusion of blacks from the grand jury that indicted him constituted racial discrimination in denial of equal protection of the law. The Court agreed; following this decision, blacks were deliberately named to grand juries. However, the impact of the demographic testimony in *Hill* was carried no further than mere token inclusion of blacks on grand juries; proportional representation was not guaranteed. Three years after *Hill*, the Supreme Court verified its approach of tokenism by affirming the rape conviction of a black man whose appeal was based on the fact that only one black sat on the grand jury (*Akins v. Texas*, 325 U.S. 398 [1945]). Supporting its decision, the Court stated:

[F]airness in selection has never been held to require proportional representation. . . . Defendants under our criminal statutes are not entitled to . . . demand representatives of their racial inheritance upon juries before whom they are tried. But . . . [they] are entitled to require that those who are trusted with jury selection shall not pursue a course of conduct which results in discrimination in the selection of jurors on racial grounds (325 U.S. 398 at 403).

Hill, *Akins*, and cases relying on the *Hill* precedent all involved appeals of Negro criminal convictions alleging discrimination in selection of either grand or petit jurors. (See, for example, *Brown v. Allen*, 344 U.S. 443 [1953]; *Collins v. Walker*, 379 U.S. 901 [1964]; *Swain v. Alabama*, 380 U.S. 202 [1965]; *Brooks v. Beto*, 366 F.2d 1 [5th Cir. 1966].) In each case, statistical evidence was presented to show the proper proportional representation and from that to argue discriminatory, disproportionate exclusion of blacks. *Hill*, demonstrating absolute exclusion, was successful. But for the arguments proving only disproportionate representation, the statistical evidence of discrimination was held insufficient. In the eyes of the Court, demography was not the most pertinent issue. Statistics were persuasive only when they proved absolute, systematic exclusion. Enforcement of proportional representation by the systematic inclusion of blacks would present yet another constitutional problem—conflict with the traditional jury system of random selection and the Sixth Amendment guarantee of trial by an impartial jury (*Swain v. Alabama*, 380 U.S. 202 at 221 [1965]; *Collins v. Walker*, 379 U.S. 901 [1964]).

COMMUNITY BIAS   On the whole, attempts to prove community bias through statistical analysis have proven futile. Courts have not found generalizations very valuable when an individual's guilt is being determined. In *Maxwell v. Bishop* (257 F. Supp. 710 [E.D. Ark. 1966], *aff'd*, 398 F.2d 138 [8th Cir. 1968], *vacated and remanded on other grounds*, 398 U.S. 262 [1970]), a black man was convicted of raping a white woman. In an attempt to prove the dangerous influence of community bias and denial of equal protection inherent in the trial, the defense presented a statistical study showing that, in Arkansas, the chances of the death sentence following a conviction of interracial rape were disproportionately higher than when rape occurred within racial lines. (See Wolfgang, *Preliminary Analysis of Rape and Capital Punishment in the State of Arkansas*, 1945-65, Exhibit for Petitioner, p. 4, *Maxwell v. Bishop*, 257 F. Supp. 710 [E.D. Ark. 1966] cited in Reiss 1970, p. 35.) But the Court was not swayed. While admitting that statistical evidence was more extensive and sophisticated than had been produced in previous trials, the court still rejected Wolfgang's study because it lacked sufficient breadth, accuracy, and precision needed "to establish satisfactorily that Arkansas juries in general practice unconstitutional racial discrimination in rape cases" (257 F. Supp. at 719). Both the district court and the court of appeals (398 F.2d 138) criticized the scope of the Wolfgang study, claiming that it did not constitute a representative sample. Indeed, Wolfgang surveyed very few counties and did not include the county of original jurisdiction. In addition, the variables were imprecisely defined; the statistics revealed very few details about the cases in which black rapists were sentenced to death.

In the view of both the district court and appellate court, the focus of Wolfgang's study was irrelevant. The issue was not death in the aggregate sense, but the determination of guilt and the appropriate punishment of the individual:

[The court] was not yet ready to condemn and upset the result reached in every case of a Negro rape defendant in the State of Arkansas on the basis of broad theories of social and statistical injustice, . . . [nor] to nullify . . . [the] petitioner's . . . trial on the basis of results generally, but elsewhere, throughout the South.

[W]hatever value it may have as an instrument of social concern . . . the statistical argument did nothing to destroy the integrity of Maxwell's trial (398 F.2d 138 at 147).

Moreover, both courts appeared outwardly hostile to statistical arguments in general. As cynically stated in the district court opinion, "statistics are elusive things at best, and it is a truism that almost anything can be proved by them" (257 F. Supp. 710 at 720).

DEATH BIAS   In *Witherspoon v. Illinois* (391 U.S. 510 [1968]), the NAACP Legal Defense and Education Fund challenged a procedure of jury selection based on whether or not the juror was bothered by the death penalty. Jurors who had no scruples against the death penalty, like those selected for the *Witherspoon* trial, were labeled death-qualified. The NAACP maintained that "such a jury, unlike the one chosen at random from a cross section of the community, must necessarily be biased in favor of conviction" (391 U.S. at 516).

As jury bias was a problem subject to evaluation only through essentially nonlegal empirical analysis, four existing social science studies were incorporated into the brief. Each study supported the hypothesis that death-qualified juries were likely to be prosecution-prone in their determination of guilt. Moreover, they proposed that death-qualified individuals were drawn disproportionately from groups whose systematic exclusion or limitation from juries was prohibited (Edison 1970, p. 55). Two of the studies were attitude analyses of college students and deemed irrelevant (Cody-Wilson and Faye-Goldberg). Only the remaining two, Robert Crosson's attitude survey of ex-jurors and Hans Zeisel's behavioral study of jurors in actual criminal cases, were considered applicable. However, due to the nature of the social science evidence, the Court concluded with strong justification that the data were "too fragmentary to establish that jurors . . . not opposed to the death penalty tend to favor the prosecution in determination of guilt. . . . [T]he exclusion of jurors opposed to capital punishment [does not conclusively] result in an unrepresentative jury . . . or substantially increase the risk of conviction" (391 U.S. 510 at 517-18).

Jury Size

In two recent decisions, the Supreme Court acknowledged another critical empirical issue: whether the reduction of the traditional 12-member jury to 6 would adversely affect trial results. In each case the Court cited empirical data as proof that it would not (Zeisel and Diamond 1974, p. 281). Based on empirical data, the decision in *Williams v. Florida* (399 U.S. 78 [1970]) upheld the use of a 6-member jury in state criminal cases. Three years later, citing both the "convincing empirical evidence" of *Williams* and four additional studies that allegedly discredited any difference between 12- and 6-member jury decisions, the Court in *Colegrove v. Battin* (413 U.S. 149 [1973]) sanctioned the use of a 6-member jury in federal civil litigation. The Court was again misled, as the four studies did not support this premise.[2] In fact, Zeisel and Diamond, noted scholars in the area of statistical legal analysis, assert that no study has produced satisfactory evidence regarding the impact of 6-member juries. However, as a consequence of the persuasiveness of the *Williams* and *Colegrove* data, over two-thirds of the federal district courts now require 6-member civil juries (Zeisel and Diamond 1974, p. 293).

Bail and Pretrial Detention—The Bellamy Memorandum

The Bellamy Memorandum, a study of the effect of pretrial detention on the outcome of a criminal case, was a rare example of social research that wielded a direct, almost immediate influence on reform (see "The Unconstitutional Administration of Bail: *Bellamy v. Judges of New York City*" [1960], cited in Hindelang 1972, p. 507). The research in the memorandum set out empirical evidence that identified the court's decision at arraignment regarding detention or release of the accused as a critical factor affecting the outcome of a case. Both the initial analysis and the consequent experimentation demonstrated that careful screening and procedural notification of defendants released without bond produced a higher percentage of court appearances than the traditional bail bond system. Those unable to make bail were substantially less likely to be cleared.

[2] These studies were conducted by Bermant and Coppock, in Washington; the Institute of Judicial Administration, in New Jersey; and the University of Michigan *Journal of Legal Reform*.

As a result, the Bellamy study was instrumental in providing a factual basis for reform. Beginning in 1966, the Vera Foundation sponsored the Manhattan Bail project—a three-year project designed to test the hypothesis of the Bellamy Memorandum. This project furnished the arraigning judge with enough verified information on the defendant's personal, financial, and community background to facilitate a knowledgeable decision regarding bail (Botein 1965, p. 326). It proved to be successful, and when the Vera funding expired, in 1966, the Office of Probation of the City of New York took it over with plans for expansion. However, soon after the project became defunct. Only recently have there been plans for its reinitiation. In fact, its success might have been greater outside of New York. In the mid-1960s, projects patterned after the Manhattan Bail project were started in Washington, D.C., St. Louis, Des Moines, and Tulsa.

Conclusion

Throughout this century, courts have been generally unreceptive to expert probability and statistical testimony. Since the use of probabilities and statistics is frequently misunderstood or incorrectly applied, the logical assumption is that the courts based their skepticism on the persistent errors in application (Cullison 1969, p. 509). Indeed, the trend in the use of statistical evidence has been one of misapplication and misinterpretation, but, until *Collins*, it went largely unnoticed by the courts. Instead, the prevailing judicial attitude was simply one of mistrust. Ironically, the recent emphasis on statistical evidence and accompanying attempts at its clarification has enhanced—not erased—this bias. Although the volume of statistical and probability evidence has grown since the 1960s, the skepticism of the courts has increased correspondingly, with legitimate justifications. Only the most specific, and consequently the most credible, evidence, like that provided in the Bellamy Memorandum, has proven useful.

PUBLIC OPINION SURVEYS

The social scientists who have testified most frequently are public opinion analysts (Greenberg 1956, p. 954). Their surveys have been introduced as fairly reliable evidence in cases dealing with antitrust, trademarks and unfair competition, government regulation, and, to a lesser extent, as evidence of community bias, primarily racial bias. Since the 1920s, public opinion surveys have aided in settling disputes between private interests and between private interests and public agencies. In many instances, public opinion polls have influenced final administrative decisions.

In antitrust cases, public opinion polls consistently have provided useful and reliable evidence—most extensively in trademark and unfair competition cases. Since it is recognized that the special trade meaning of a word or symbol in the eyes of the public is a matter of fact, the most appropriate test is the measurement of public reaction. Data in public survey polls provide a relatively objective means of determining the likelihood of public confusion.

The reception of early trademark survey evidence, however, was highly inconsistent. At times the evidence was ruled inadmissible hearsay and flatly rejected; as such, it was judged as an out-of-court statement, offered for the truth of its content and not falling within one of the many exceptions to the hearsay rule of evidence. Frequently, the issue of admissability turned on very fine distinctions. To illustrate, surveys were excluded as hearsay in *Elgin National Watch Co. v. Elgin Clock Co.* (26 F.2d 376 [D. Del. 1928]) because the affidavit presenting the questionnaire that interpreted the survey results was not based on the affiant's personal knowledge. But similar surveys were admitted in *Del Monte Special Food Co. v. California Packing Corp.* (34 F.2d 774 [9th Cir. 1929]) because the investigator's testimony was limited to relating the confusion of the interviewees. In *Buckeye Soda Co. v. Oakite Products* (U.S. Pat. Quart. 152, *aff'd*, 19 Cust. & Pat. App. 1034, 56 F.2d 462 [1930]), a trademark confusion survey was admitted but denied probative weight. In each of these cases, the survey methods were similar; what differed was the means of presentation to the courts. The *Elgin* investigator testified to the personal knowledge of third parties, who were not present at trial and thus not available for cross-examination; his evidence was not admitted. In contrast, the testimony of the *Del Monte* investigator was based on his personal observation of the confusion of the third parties; his evidence was admitted.

By current standards, the probative weight attached to a survey corresponds directly with its technical adequacy. *Standard Oil Co. v. Standard Oil Co.* (252 F.2d 65 [10th Cir. 1958]) stands as the leading case defining the admissibility of public opinion trademark surveys. The *Standard Oil* court held that "results of a public recognition survey may be received to establish whether trade symbols in question have achieved a degree of public recognition that constitutes secondary meaning and as to whether there is confusing similarity in designations" among trademark symbols (252 F.2d 65, 75).

Opinion polls also serve as an accurate demonstration of public reaction in government regulation cases. For example, in *Rhodes Pharmaceutical Co. v. F.T.C.* (208 F.2d 382 [7th Cir. 1953]), the appellant successfully used a public opinion survey demonstrating public interpretation of his advertisement to rebut a charge of false and misleading advertising. Even in government regulation cases, the survey must be technically accurate and objective. In keeping with this criterion, the *United States v. 38 Doz. Bottles* (114 F. Supp. 461 [D.C. Minn. 1953]) court considered the results of a formal survey conducted by an expert in advertising and marketing psychology but refused to admit two more informal surveys conducted by private advertisers.

Moreover, public opinion surveys have also been focused on less tangible concerns, notably the determination of community bias to support motions for change of venue. By definition, this category implies a less quantifiable measurement of human reaction and a much stronger involvement of value judgments. Consequently, it has not been accorded a high degree of probative weight (Greenberg 1956, p. 962). Although the absence of social research dealing with community sentiment was noted as early as 1940—when a federal court of appeals needed to define the legal test of good moral character (*Repouille v. United States*, 165 F.2d 152 [2d Cir. 1947])—the use of such research has lagged. Only recently has it gained momentum.

United States v. Hiss (185 F.2d 822 [1950], *cert. denied*, 340 U.S. 948) was one of the earliest attempts to use public opinion surveys to prove community bias, but the evidence did not persuade the court. The federal court of appeals denied the defendant's motion for change of venue, which was based on comparisons of community bias in New York City and Rutland, Vermont. Similar denial of poll evidence occurred in *Irvin v. State* (66 So. 2d 288 [Fla. 1953], *cert. denied sub nom. Irvin v. Florida*, 346 U.S. 927 [1954], *reh. denied*, 347 U.S. 914). Irvin, a black man, was accused of raping a white woman. His attorneys engaged the Roper firm to investigate the extent of community bias in hopes of supporting a motion for change of venue (see 66 So. 2d at 290-91). The Supreme Court of Florida, however, rejected the poll evidence as "informal and largely based on hearsay [going] . . . far beyond the latitude allowed by the statute and . . . established procedure" (66 So. 2d at 291). Moreover, the court questioned the poll's objectivity and competence, stating that "neither of the witnesses had more than a vicarious knowledge of what occurred in the interviews"—and even noting the Roper firm's incorrect predictions in the 1948 elections!

However, the courts' attitudes have changed. More recent cases have used public opinion surveys in conjunction with statistical analysis and social psychological research to win motions for change of venue (e.g., *Furman v. Georgia*, 408 U.S. 238 [1972]; *Williams v. Florida*, 399 U.S. 78 [1970]; *State v. Little*, 286 N.C. 185 [1975]). Presently in criminal law, research in support of change of venue is the most influential social science data. In light of the belief that a jury should represent a random sample of the population, the courts recognize that the potential danger of reflecting community prejudice in the attitudes of jury members does exist. Thus, in these situations the probability is very high that the generalizations will apply to the sample.

Conclusion

Currently, many attorneys use public opinion surveys, and courts are frequently required to judge their admissibility. Judicial reception is not universal; it varies among courts, geographical locations, and, with the greatest disparity, among subject areas. As the focus of a survey shifts from the specific, such as reaction to advertising, to the more intangible, subjective reactions, such as community racial bias, the skepticism of the courts increases sharply.

Three factors explain this disparity in judicial attitude. First is the question of accuracy; in the view of many judges, the sample basis taints the survey's reliability and comprehensiveness. Second is the question of method. Undeniably, the analysis of survey evidence requires the evaluation of hearsay statements. Even when presented during expert testimony (which in itself is arguably inappropriate as it is not the best evidence available), the analysis of out-of-court statements, filtered through the expert's own opinions, risks the danger of bias and distortions. The third factor is cost. Because survey research is expensive, it is logical that an attorney with a limited amount of research money will give investment in legal research first priority.

Clearly, the predominant barrier to judicial acceptance, upon which the two others hinge, is mistrust of the survey's accuracy. The courts have struggled with this doubt since survey evidence was first used. Over time, they have refined the solution, choosing to focus on the relative appropriateness of hearsay evidence and the practical inconvenience involved in providing firsthand reports. In *G&C Merriam Co. v. Syndicate Publishing Co.* (207 Fed. 515, 518 [2d Cir. 1913], *appeal dismissed*, 237 U.S. 618), Judge Learned Hand stated, "the requisites of an exception of the hearsay rule [are] necessity and circumstantial guarantee of trustworthiness." Later, the criteria for acceptance were expanded to include evidence exclusively provided by surveys:

[O]pinion testimony by an acceptable expert resting wholly or partly on information, oral or documentary, recited by him as gathered from others, which [was] . . . trustworthy and . . . practically unobtainable by other means, . . . [was] competent even though the first hand sources from which the information came [could] not be produced in court (*United States v. Aluminum Co. of America*, 35 F. Supp. 820 at 823 [S.D.N.Y. 1940]).

American Luggage Works v. United States Trunk Co. (158 F. Supp. 50 [D. Mass. 1957], *aff'd sub nom. Hawley Products Co. v. United States Trunk Co.*, 259 F.2d 69 [1st Cir. 1958]) further defined the criteria, admitting survey evidence if the risks of distortion were minimized.

Over time, the development of a workable rationale for determining an acceptable degree of accuracy gave rise to use of the "state-of-mind" doctrine. Hearsay evidence is now tolerated when it is submitted solely to express a general public reaction, or when it reflects the state of mind of the interviewers who are present in court. But statements of the persons interviewed are not tolerated when offered primarily for the truth contained in their individual opinions (*United States v. 88 Cases*, 187 F.2d 967, 974 [3d Cir. 1951], *cert. denied*, 342 U.S. 861 [1951]; Zeisel 1959, p. 335).

Beyond the technical barrier posed by the rules of evidence, there is a second, often more formidable, obstacle to acceptance of survey evidence—the legal emphasis on protection of the individual. Because of this predisposition, research evidence that merely purports to describe the societal context will be admitted much more easily than generalizations that bear directly upon an individual's fate. Thus, within the category of evidence protected by the state-of-mind doctrine, surveys focusing on specific, relatively objective public reactions, such as government regulations and public confusion of trademarks, are more readily accepted than those evaluating more subjective topics such as segregation, education, and racial bias. Although potentially applicable, the state-of-mind doctrine is only beginning to influence the admission of evidence in more socially explosive areas.

PSYCHOLOGICAL RESEARCH

Court treatment of psychological evidence pertaining to criminal cases has been, at best, erratic. For over a century, the standard by which mentally ill persons were judged criminally responsible was derived from nineteenth century English law (*M'Naghten's Case*, X Clark & Finnelly 200, at 208 *et seq.*, 8 Eng. Rep. 718, 722 H.L. [1843]), which defined criminal responsibility as a function of *mens rea*, or criminal intent. To a great degree, the *M'Naghten* standard requiring a person's knowledge of both the nature of the act and its quality of wrongness still applies.

However, there have been intermittent departures from this approach. One of the more bizarre tangents taken by criminal law occurred in the 1920s; unfortunately, it was based on social research. Social scientists in the 1920s entertained the theory that society's evils, particularly crime, were traceable to feeblemindedness. Indeed, this was believed to be the basis of most criminality. Famous studies purported to show that one feebleminded parent, who lived in the late 1700s, had through his offspring produced thousands of delinquents. Based on these studies, state legislation provided for the sterilization of feebleminded people (Kramer 1959, p. 567). And when challenged, these laws were upheld by the Supreme Court in *Buck v. Bell* (274 U.S. 200 at 207 [1927]). Writing for the majority, Justice Oliver Wendell Holmes stated:

We have seen more than once that the public welfare may call upon the best citizens for their lives. It would be strange if it could not call upon those who already sap the strength of the state for these lesser sacrifices, often not felt to be such by those concerned in order to prevent our being swamped with incompetence. It is better for all the world if instead of waiting to execute degenerate offspring for crime or to let them starve for their imbecility, society can prevent those who are manifestly unfit from continuing their kind.

Shortly thereafter, the theory was successfully challenged; new studies discredited the theory that feeblemindedness was the basis for criminality. The actions prior to and including the *Buck* decision were strongly reminiscent of the Salem witch trials—the difference being that the more contemporary action was carried out with the sanctions of social research. However, this example is aberrational.

The past two decades have witnessed a heightened sensitivity toward mental incompetence and, with that, a growing awareness of the role of psychological factors in criminality. As a result, although not yet universally accepted, psychological input in legal cases is steadily gaining respectability. More recently developed tests for determining criminal responsibility based on psychological research have included the irresistible impulse test (*Argent v. United States*, 325 F.2d 162, 172 [5th Cir. 1963]), a test for the presence of a mental defect that renders the defendant incapable of conformity to law (*United States v. Currens*, 290 F.2d 751 [3d Cir. 1961]), and the diminished responsibility test (*People v. Gorshin*, 57 Cal. 2d 716, 336 P.2d 492 [1959]). In addition, many cases have admitted expert psychological testimony to aid in establishing mental competency in accordance with the standard first enunciated in *Durham v. United States* (214 F.2d 862 [D.C. Cir. 1954]). *Durham* held that a defendant whose acts were the consequences of a mental defect was not criminally responsible.

In general, attorneys remain highly skeptical of expert testimony regarding the prediction of dangerousness, considering it imprecise and potentially capable of condemning innocent people. At the crux of the legal argument against psychological research is a desire to guard against unwarranted intrusion into the human mind. Although lawyers recognize the evaluatory function of psychology in describing behavior on an aggregate scale, for the most part they deny its predictive ability with respect to individual behavior. This criticism finds justification in the fact that not even 50 percent of the psychological predictions of dangerousness are accurate.

SOCIOLOGICAL AND SOCIAL PSYCHOLOGICAL RESEARCH

Exclusive use of sociological evidence is rare; more frequently, it is used in conjunction with psychological evidence. And in light of the controversial nature of social science research, this is an altogether logical approach. Psychology, a more scientific discipline dealing with individual behavior, when placed in a sociological context will yield more comprehensive and more credible evidence. As may be expected, social psychological evidence exhibits the most extensive range of input to court cases. First used to expose the detrimental personality effects of segregation and later to prove discrimination, sociological research has in the past 20 years successfully laid the basis for many arguments of equal protection. Indeed, the National Association for the Advancement of Colored People (NAACP), which consistently incorporated sociological evidence in substantiation of its allegations of Fourteenth Amendment violations, has been its most loyal and most successful advocate.

The Brown Decision

In the area of segregation, *Brown v. Board of Education* (347 U.S. 483 [1954]; consolidated with *Briggs v. Elliot, Davis v. County School Board of Prince Edward County*, and *Gebhart v. Belton*) is considered a landmark for two reasons. First, it laid the legal foundation for a national integration policy. Second, it stands, particularly in the eyes of many social scientists, as one of the first examples of social theory that found its way into formal law. The famed footnote 11 to the majority opinion, which relied heavily on the research of sociologist Kenneth Clark, stands as the most widely renowned legal use of social research (347 U.S. 483 at 494, n.11).[3] In fact, it is widely believed within the social science community that, due to their legitimizing effects, sociological and psychological studies beginning with *Brown* acted as catalysts for the social changes of the past two decades. Since *Brown*, when the contact theory became an officially sanctioned policy model, social science research "has been inextricably interwoven with policy decisions" (Armour 1972, p. 93). Ironically, close examination of the validity of the social science evidence in *Brown*, its role in the Court's decision, and its impact on the overall process of desegregation exposes many fallacies that both the social science community and the public accepted. (See Cahn 1955 for criticism of the Clark data.)

Clark's research allegedly demonstrated the harmful effects of racial discrimination on the personalities of black children and, subsequently, on society. In his experiments, he presented black children with two dolls, identical except for skin color. One was white; the other was black. After ascertaining that the child had a clear concept of the meaning of colored, he asked which doll they preferred, or which was the "nice" doll. Two-thirds of the children tested preferred the white doll, considered it nice, and rejected the brown doll. All of these children gave spontaneous explanations of their choices, which, when categorized, reflected existing stereotypes about Negroes. The brown doll was dirty, it was going to fight, or, quite simply, it was bad. Finally Clark asked them to show him the doll they resembled. Despite their knowledge that the brown doll was colored, many said they believed themselves to be like the white doll (Clinard 1951). Others were more disturbed. In his testimony in *Davis v. County School Board of Prince Edward County* (347 U.S. 483 [1954], Clark reported:

[A] great many of the children react as if I were the devil in hell, myself, when I ask this final question. Some of them break down and leave the testing station; they cry. Particularly this is true of children in the north. It is as if I had tricked them. We were all friendly before, . . . and then I put them on the spot. . . . The explosion . . . [is] the degree to which this method . . . puts its finger upon the flagrant damage to the self esteem . . . of the Negro child (*Davis v. County School Board of Prince Edward County*, Transcript of Record at 252, filed July 12, 1952, case consolidated with *Brown v. Board of Education* on appeal to Supreme Court).

---

[3] See Allport 1953 for the appendix to the appellant's briefs in the school segregation cases prepared by psychiatrists and social scientists regarding the harmful effects of segregation on Negro school children.

Clark interpreted these results as indicative of the basic distorting personality effect of prejudice, discrimination, and segregation. He acknowledged that a number of factors, such as security, social class, and parental education level, would affect the child's reaction. But he attributed to segregation the basic conflict between the children's concepts of themselves as blacks and their self images as individuals. (*Davis v. County School Board of Prince Edward County*, Record at 252; testimony in *Briggs v. Elliot*, 347 U.S. 497). Although many believe his conclusions today, at the time his subjective method and apparent lack of sophistication in technique cast doubt upon the technical validity of his research.

Clark claimed that the South Carolina study was consistent with a similar 1947 study in which he compared the reactions of black children in the integrated schools of Springfield, Massachusetts, with black children in the segregated schools of Hot Springs, Pine Bluff, and Little Rock, Arkansas. In so doing, however, he was comparing two totally dissimilar sets. More accurate analysis would have required comparing not two but four sets of reactions—those of northern segregated, northern integrated, southern segregated, and southern integrated children. Moreover, as reported, his evidence was misrepresentative (Garfinkel 1959):

Close examination revealed that more northern than southern blacks preferred the white doll, considered the white doll nice, designated the brown doll as bad and considered the white doll like themselves. In other words, the children in integrated schools showed a higher incidence of the very reactions which Clark cited in his testimony as evidence of the harmful effects on segregated children.

Strictly from a legal point of view, the Clark data bore no direct relevance to the case at hand. As pointed out by Cahn (1955), Clark's study did not purport to measure the effects of school segregation; rather, it measured the impact of segregation in general. At best this still remained subjective and not amenable to precise measurement. Isolation of the impact of school segregation from the general effects of societal conditions is difficult if not impossible, and, considering the ages of the children tested, school segregation might reasonably be assumed to be the weaker factor. Indeed, Clark testified that the unexpected, fascinating result of his research was the realization that the ego damage occurred so early. This early detection points to sources outside the schools. Granted, school segregation would reinforce and perpetuate the damage, but that aspect was not the ostensible point of the research.

Regardless of its direct relevance, the Clark research was persuasive and only the extent of its influence is left to speculation. One thing is clear. Although it was used to support the conclusions that "separate educational facilities are inherently unequal" (347 U.S. at 498), social science research was not the prime determinant in the outcome of the case. The majority opinion in *Brown v. Board of Education* explicitly states that the decision was based on grounds of equal protection afforded by the Fourteenth Amendment (347 U.S. at 495). At most, social research in the *Brown* case was used to buttress, not to formulate, the overturn of the separate-but-equal doctrine.

Theories abound as to the exact purpose of the use of the Clark research in *Brown*, but the secrecy that cloaks Supreme Court actions precludes the determination of any definite role. Quite plausibly, the social research could have served as a political placebo. Passed off as an objective basis for such a revolutionary decision, the Court could have merely injected the research to soothe the public mind and remove part of the blame from the Court. Alternatively, the changes in the Court between the initial argument of *Brown* in 1952 and its reargument one year later may yield a clue. Within this time span, the character of the Court had shifted. Chief Justice Vinson had died; Earl Warren had succeeded him. And the Court by a very narrow margin had assumed a more liberal position. In this perspective, it is possible that the social research influenced the swing vote—if not by its content, by its potential public role as justifier.

Finally, the legal precedents involved, coupled with the carefully developed strategy of the NAACP, shed an interesting light on the role of the research. Not only did the *Brown* decision overrule the separate-but-equal doctrine, but it gave the use of social science research in legal cases its big splash. Both results were the culmination of carefully developed trends; neither was without historical precedent. Many have argued that the social research was superfluous to the actual decision; others have proposed that it provided the final push needed for the overruling of *Plessy v. Ferguson* (163 U.S. 537 [1896]). In fact, it was both the nature of the Clark information and its timing that provided the final impetus for reform.

Investigation of the precedents to *Brown* reveals a carefully constructed foundation that at first glance would condemn social research as unnecessary. *Missouri ex rel. Gaines v. Canada* (305 U.S. 337 [1938]) dealt with the inferiority of a state-supported black law school. The briefs presented strictly legal equal-protection arguments; no social science data was cited. The Court held that, regardless of whether it was separate, the state of Missouri must furnish legal education to blacks equal to that provided to whites. Ten years later,

Sipuel, a black, applied to the all-white state law school and was rejected. In *Sipuel v. Board of Regents of Oklahoma* (332 U.S. 631 [1948]), the Court held that this rejection from the only available school was in violation of equal protection. Again, there was no use of social science research.

However, further inspection reveals that, beginning with *McLaurin v. Oklahoma State Regents* (339 U.S. 637 [1950]) and *Sweatt v. Painter* (339 U.S. 629 [1950]), social science evidence was an important factor. In both of these cases, although a separate black school existed, it was inferior to the white school. Blacks who were denied admission to the white schools refused to enter the black school and sued. Expert social science evidence supporting their arguments in *Sweatt* asserted that there was no scientific evidence of intellectual inferiority determined by race, thus racial classification for educational purposes was arbitrary (*Sweatt v. Painter*, Brief for Petitioner at 24). Second, segregation prevented both black and white students from obtaining full knowledge of the separated group and consequently stimulated mutual hostility. Third, prejudice was not a congenital instinct; thus it was the very act of segregation that perpetuated group isolation and undercut social stability (Brief at 26). Fourth, segregation accentuated the imagined differences between blacks and whites, creating an atmosphere unfavorable to proper education and stifling the black child's motivation to learn. "A definitive study of the scientific works of contemporary sociologists, historians, and anthropologists conclusively document[s] the proposition that the intent and result of [segregation is] . . . the establishment of an inferior status" (Brief for Petitioner at 28). Asserting that this status was neither valid, necessary, nor societally advantageous, the petitioners argued that it should be eliminated. The Court accepted their propositions holding that, since the education offered by the black law school was substantially inferior, the Fourteenth Amendment required that blacks be admitted to the white law school. On its face, the *Sweatt* evidence appears strong enough to have supported the *Brown* decision, perhaps stronger than the Clark data actually used. Assuming the strength of the *Sweatt* precedent, the Clark data of *Brown* appears to be more a justifying than a persuasive factor.

Whether the intended role of social science research in the school segregation cases was to buttress or to exert influence on its own merits, its deliberate presence cannot be denied. Clearly, the NAACP had laid a careful foundation for *Brown*. They had struggled for 16 years to convince the Supreme Court that segregation was in violation of the Fourteenth Amendment; precedents to *Brown* contained both legal and social science arguments. The NAACP strategy in educational segregation cases had begun with higher education, in particular with legal education (*Missouri ex rel. Gaines v. Canada*), and progressed to the elementary level, culminating in the *Brown* decision. It appeared that they made little headway so long as their arguments were framed purely in separate-but-equal terms, such as size of classes, length of school terms, salaries of teachers, physical conditions of the school, or distance required to travel. It has been suggested by Will Maslow, Director of the Commission on Law and Social Action of the American Jewish Congress (Cahn 1955, p. 157), that it was only when the issue became one of the damage to student morale as a result of federally imposed segregation that the Court became interested:

When the final decision was handed down in the public school segregation cases, it rested not on conceptual legal principles or the legislative history of the Fourteenth Amendment or even on the sociological demonstration that in practice segregation results in inferior schools but on the psychological finding of thwarted intellectual development.

In the years following *Brown*, the courts probed the area of segregation; accordingly, the scope of segregation litigation expanded. Cases progressed from ruling against segregation in schools per se (*Brown v. Board of Education*) to upholding school busing programs (*Keyes v. School District No. 1*, 413 U.S. 189 [1973]), contesting the unfair educational consequences of school tracking systems (*Hobson v. Hansen*, 269 F. Supp. 401, 495 (D.D.C. 1967), aff'd sub nom. *Smuck v. Hobson*, 408 F.2d 175 [D.C. Cir. 1969]), standardized testing (*Chance v. Board of Examiners*, 330 F. Supp. 203 [S.D.N.Y. 1971]), and reevaluating school financing procedures (*Serrano v. Priest*, 5 Cal. 3d 584, 487 P.2d 1241, 96 Cal. Rptr. 601 [1971], 45 U.S.L.W. 2340, June 30, 1976). Moreover, the controversy sparked by the *Brown* decision generated its own demand for research. Consequently, relying on the *Brown* precedent and the ensuing boom in research, the arguments in cases after *Brown* frequently cited social science studies.

The Coleman Report

In the early 1960s, Congress commissioned the U.S. Office of Education to conduct a survey concerning the lack of public educational opportunities due to race, color, religion, or national origin. Known as the Coleman Report (Coleman *et al.* 1966), the report stressed two main points. First, the single greatest determinant of a child's academic performance is family background. And, second, if a minority pupil from a home lacking educational strength studies with schoolmates having strong educational backgrounds, the minority child's achievement level will improve—without effecting a negative response in the performance of the other children. Thus, increasing contact between white and minority students, from a purely educational viewpoint, was not a zero-sum operation. Coleman's "contact theory" predicted that the achievements and aspirations of black students should improve in direct proportion to the increased contact between black and white students, and the performance of white children would not suffer.

The publication of the Coleman Report in 1966 gave fresh impetus to the desegregation drive, which had been stymied by years of southern intransigence (Ravitch 1975). In particular, civil rights groups seized on Coleman's second point in advocating integration through the busing of school children. As a result, the Coleman Report strongly influenced the issuance of the federal busing order of 1970 and was persuasive in subsequent litigation (see *Keyes v. School District No. 1*, 413 U.S. 189 [1973]; *Swann v. Board of Education*, 402 U.S. 1 [1970]; *Brewer v. School Board of City of Norfolk, Virginia*, 434 F.2d 408 [4th Cir. 1970]; *Brunson v. Board of Trustees of School District No. 1*, 429 F.2d 820 [4th Cir. 1970]).

However, the busing experiment has not achieved the success that the Coleman research projected. At present, there are widespread doubts regarding its overall effectiveness. The current debate turns on two particular issues: whether busing stimulates white flight from city public schools to suburbs and private schools, and whether it has educational value for black pupils. It is now apparent that the research on which the busing actions relied so heavily suffered from a far too limited scope, focusing solely on the positive impact on children but abstracting the potentially negative reactions of adults. Ironically, nine years after his original report, Coleman laid the blame not on the research, but on the courts' use of his research, claiming in an April 1975 address that: "in an area such as school desegregation, which has important consequences for individuals, and in which individuals retain control of some actions that can in the end defeat the policy, the courts are probably the worst instrument of social policy."

Educational Tracking

By the 1970s social research had finally come into its own; it was no longer uncommon to have social science evidence supporting the arguments of both parties to a lawsuit. *Hobson v. Hansen*, one of the first educational tracking cases, was such a case. The briefs of both sides incorporated extensive social science research dealing with the segregative and educational impacts of tracking. The issues raised required the court not only to resolve the question of equal protection but, more significantly, to evaluate the scientific competence of the tracking system. Holding against tracking, the opinion stated that, although ability grouping is an accepted educational practice, the IQ tests upon which it was based did not reliably measure the innate abilities of minority students. Since IQ tests were standardized on white middle-class children, disadvantaged minority children were unfairly relegated to lower tracks. Thus, they received an education inferior to that of whites in violation of their Fourteenth Amendment rights (see also *Johnson v. San Francisco Unified School District*, 339 F. Supp. 1315 [N.D. Cal. 1971]).

Larry P. v. Riles (343 F. Supp. 1306 [N.D. Cal. 1972]) went a step further, challenging the teaching misclassification of black children as educably mentally retarded. Relying on the findings of *Hobson* and socio-psychological evidence of a statistical racial imbalance in IQ testing, the brief for Larry P. alleged that the IQ tests that were a substantial factor in placement yielded a disproportionate classification of black children as mentally retarded. And, introducing the "null hypothesis of special education," it proposed that failure to prove a relationship between race and intelligence requires the assumption that no relationship exists. On this basis, the court held that the disproportionate classification of blacks as educably mentally retarded was unconstitutionally discriminatory.

Standardized Testing for Employment

The case against standardized testing was carried into the employment arena in the early 1970s. Again, social science played a role in resolving the validity of these tests. Unlike the education cases, which involved allegations of deprivations of constitutional rights, employment discrimination cases required statutory interpretation as well. Title VII §703 of the Civil Rights Act of 1964 forbids an employer to classify or segregate employees or limit their production to deprive them of employment opportunities or adversely affect their status because of race, color, religion, sex, or national origin. But §703(h) authorizes the use of any professionally developed employee aptitude test provided it is not designed, intended, or used to discriminate. Bohrer (1973, p. 383) comments:

> While the question of what constitutes a rational relationship between the methods and the purpose of classification has not been definitively answered by the courts, the procedures used to evaluate standardized tests have been continually refined. The employment test cases reveal the key factors in the

evaluation of standardized tests: their discriminatory impact and the usefulness of the tests to employers.

The leading case on this topic was *Griggs v. Duke Power Company* (401 U.S. 424 [1971]). Relying on a statistical study, the plaintiffs convinced the court that standardized tests used as an employment criterion failed to predict job success or measure job-related abilities and placed blacks at a marked disadvantage in the labor market. The Court held that employment tests must indicate a "demonstrably reasonable measure of job performance" (401 U.S. 436). Thus, any employment practice excluding blacks that cannot be shown to be related to job performance was prohibited, notwithstanding the employer's lack of discriminatory intent (see also *Armstead v. Starkville Municipal Separate School District*, 325 F. Supp. 560 [N.D. Miss. 1971], *modified*, 461 F.2d 276 [5th Cir. 1972]).

In *Chance v. Board of Examiners* (330 F. Supp. 203 [S.D.N.Y. 1971], *aff'd*, 458 F.2d 1167 [2d Cir. 1972]), another challenge to standardized employment tests, neither party initially presented social science evidence. But skeptical of the plaintiff's ability to prove their claims of discriminatory practice, the trial court "ordered [each] . . . party to develop a survey to determine comparative pass rates of different ethnic groups in recent years" (458 F.2d 1167 at 1171). Based on the evidence subsequently presented, the court issued an injunction against both future exams and licensing based on previous exams. The defendant board of examiners appealed, challenging the trial court's use of statistics, but the judgment of the court below was affirmed.

School Financing

In the landmark decision of *Serrano v. Priest*, the Supreme Court of California relied on the statistical and socioeconomic research of Coons, Clune, and Sugarman in striking down the traditional means of support for local school systems—local property taxes (see, 57 Cal. L. Rev. 388). Following an analysis of the total assessed valuation of real estate, amount of money spent per pupil, local variations in property tax rates, and state contributions to student costs, the court concluded that regional variations in income and property values, as identified, yielded regional fluctuation in the quality of education. The subsequent inability of poorer districts to sustain an educational level comparable to that of the more wealthy districts was a denial of equal protection. Thus, the court concluded that:

[T]he California public school financing system, with its substantial dependence on local property taxes and resultant wide disparities in school revenue, violates the equal protection clause of the Fourteenth Amendment. . . . [T]his funding scheme invidiously discriminates against the poor because it makes the quality of a child's education a function of the wealth of his parents and neighbors (5 Cal. 3d at 589, 96 Cal. Rptr. 601 at 604).

Serrano marked the start of a national trend eliminating state reliance on local property taxes as the principal means of financing public schools. Since the *Serrano* decision, 19 states have legislated major school financing reforms. Eight others have assumed larger shares of the burden of education. And persuaded by *Serrano*, state courts in New Jersey, Washington, and Connecticut have held state property tax financing systems unconstitutional because of the inequities created between rich and poor districts. Each court delegated the responsibility for developing a replacement system to the state legislatures. To date, only the New Jersey legislature, which passed a state income tax for school financing in 1976, has completed its reform measures (Sullivan, N.Y.T., April 20, 1976; see N.J. Stat. Ann. 18A:7A-2, -4 [Supp. 1976]).

But the battle stopped at the Supreme Court. Faced with analogous contentions and presented with similar supporting social science data, the United States Supreme Court arrived at a conclusion opposite to *Serrano*. In *Rodriquez v. San Antonio Independent School District* (411 U.S. 1 [1973]), the court dismissed the equal protection contention on the grounds that there was no fundamental right to education. Thus, only absolute denial of educational opportunities would trigger the protection of the Fourteenth Amendment. But there was no "interference with fundamental rights where only relative differences in spending levels [were] . . . involved and where . . . no charge fairly could be made that the system fails to provide each child with an opportunity to acquire the basic minimal skills necessary for the enjoyment of the rights of speech and of full participation in the political process" (411 U.S. at 37). As in the jury representation cases, the Court retreated to an absolutist position in deference to more pervasive constitutional standards—irrespective of any supra-legal proof that might compel a contrary holding. It stated that to hold otherwise would require the Court to "intrude in an area which it has traditionally deferred to state legislature (411 U.S. at 40)" and assume a role for which the Court lacks both authority and competence (411 U.S. at 54).

Other Cases

Although the primary focus of sociological-psychological evidence used in the past two decades has been segregation in education and employment, this has not been its sole application. Sociological evidence combined with the testimony of anthropologist Solomon Katz substantiated the overrule of Virginia's antimiscegenation laws (*Loving v. Commonwealth of Virginia*, 388 U.S. 1 [1967]). The works of child psychologists and sociologists concerning the moral and intellectual age of maturity were noted in Justice Douglas's dissent in the Amish compulsory education case, *Wisconsin v. Yoder* (405 U.S. 205 at 245, note 3, citing Piaget, Elkind, Kohlberg, Kay, Gessell, and Ilg). Herein Douglas inferred that the majority court should have paid closer attention to these studies in its determination of the age of legal responsibility. And testimony regarding the occupational, employment, and educational status of blacks given by sociologist Arnold M. Rose persuaded the court to give a black father custody of his mulatto child in *Morse v. Fields* (127 F. Supp. 63 [S.D.N.Y. 1954]).

One of the newest subjects of sociological-psychological research deals with the extent of the "chilling effect" on First Amendment freedoms resulting from government surveillance of social dissidents. Although still in its early stages, surveillance research and its attempt to determine the severity of chill necessary to evoke judicial remedy may be significant in the future in defining the legal limits of government intrusion. Of the many surveillance cases of the past 15 years, only two have used social research. In each case the research was persuasive, although, in view of the circumstances, the victories were limited.

The decision in *Keyishian v. Board of Regents* (385 U.S. 589 [1967]) outlawing the required anti-Communist pledge for New York State teachers overruled the 1952 decision of *Adler v. Board of Education* (342 U.S. 485 [1952]). However, the use of the social research in *Keyishian* was not so monumental as it may appear. First, *Adler* was decided without the benefit of social science research in the midst of the McCarthy era—in an atmosphere that would have smothered the *Keyishian* type of evidence. In retrospect, the shifting social context may have been more responsible for the new decision than the social science evidence. Second, the *Keyishian* evidence stands as a prime example of misdirected social science research. In evaluating the "chilling effect" on the New York teachers, the *Keyishian* study neglected to analyze the effects of the New York pledge legislation, which had been in operation for the 15 years since *Adler*. In short, it failed to deal with the impact of the very legislation that it alleged to be unconstitutional.

More recently, the plaintiff's brief in *Tatum v. Laird* (408 U.S. 1 [1972]) included a lengthy appendix detailing psychological and

sociological evidence that verified the existence of the chill phenomenon inherent in government surveillance programs. Despite the government's arguments that the claim of chill was too hypothetical, the
court remanded the case for retrial—expressly to determine the severity of chill created. On the issue of surveillance, the court agreed that
social research was relevant, as surveillance was a social matter
affecting individual rights.

In sum, the effective use of social research in the segregation cases
paved the way for a much broader use of social research. As has been
shown, sociological-legal research is no longer confined to determining
racial bias. It is now used in a wide and expanding range of cases—with
increasing success. The opinion of the court in *Parham v. South
Western Bell Telephone Co.* (433 F.2d 421 [8th Cir. 1970]) indicates the
new position of sociological research in a niche so effectively carved by
the segregation and discrimination issues:

In cases concerning racial discrimination, "statistics often tell much and
Courts listen." . . . The statistical evidence introduced by Parham clearly
demonstrated the Company's discriminatory employment practices from July
2, 1965, until February 1967.
. . . We hold as a matter of law that these statistics which revealed an
extraordinarily small number of black employees, except for the most part as
menial laborers, established a violation of the Title VII of the Civil Rights Act
of 1964 (433 F.2d 421 at 426, citations deleted).

FORCES AFFECTING THE GROWTH OF SOCIOLEGAL COOPERATION

The application of social science research to legal problems has gained
a strong foothold throughout the course of this century. Particularly in
the last decade, the use of sociolegal research has intensified and
branched out into more controversial, less quantifiable topics. Attorneys and judges have begun to view legal issues neither in isolation nor
in a vacuum, but in the more comprehensive framework of conditions
revealed by the social sciences. In perspective, however, this development represents only the first step. Upon analysis, three forces
appear to be the major hindrances to social science-legal cooperation.
Foremost is the intellectual strain between lawyers and social scientists. More subtle are the political context within which social science
and the law must interact and the time lag between the results of
research by social scientists and their effects on the attitudes of
society.

APPREHENSION OF THE LEGAL PROFESSION

Above all, the profound differences in perspective between social scientists and lawyers have laid an unstable foundation for the alliance between social science and law. The legal focus on remedies for individual clients presents both a strength and a weakness. "The strength is . . . individualized justice. . . . The weakness is that they sometimes treat only part of the problem and do not touch more basic issues" (Handler 1971, pp. 346, 347). Indeed, both in research and in resolution, the legal approach is much narrower than the scientific. Ideally, cooperation with social science would expand this relatively narrow scope.

There still remains a skepticism verging on hostility that pervades the legal attitude toward social science—a condition that in turn frustrates attempts to use social science research. It has been suggested that the single most important barrier to the use of social science evidence is ignorance (Lochner 1973). In practice, this contention gains merit. As most lawyers lack social science training, they are frequently incapable of evaluating sophisticated social science research. Consequently, their attitudes range from highly skeptical to uncritically receptive, although on the whole the skepticism prevails. But there are dangers inherent to either position. The skeptics, who substantiate their criticism with examples of unreliable research such as the misrepresentation of the *Brown* evidence or the lack of statistical precision in *Collins*, tend to discount the validity of the social science evidence automatically or disregard it entirely. At the other extreme, those who blindly use evidence without bothering to evaluate it critically risk perpetuating unsound research. If research is not scrutinized upon its initial use, mistakes that survived the first evaluation may survive each successive use, since previously used studies tend to receive only cursory legal review.

The recent inception of social science programs in many law schools is beginning to solve this problem. As a result, some new lawyers now enter the profession equipped with the analytical skills of the social sciences, particularly economics, in addition to those of law. But the skepticism of social science that pervades the legal profession reaches down to the ranks of the students as well, retarding the positive effect of their training. Morever, this positive effect will cut both ways. More thorough understanding of social science analysis will erase some of the inherent prejudice against social science, but it will also expose the analytical and methodological problems in the research.

Generally, the skepticism of the legal profession stems not from analytical handicaps but from sheer mistrust. In part this is a sensible reaction. Lawyers are skeptical, frequently justifiably, of the alleged "extravagant claims of . . . psychiatrists that every criminal is simply a sick individual who, given psychiatric treatment would be made sane . . . [or of] sociologists that every criminal is simply a product of his environment and if you will change this environment, you will have an honest, law abiding citizen" (Gibbons 1971, p. 151).

Moreover, many lawyers frequently condemn social science as overly dependent on value judgments and empirically unverifiable. Critical of the malleability of social science evidence, they question its accuracy and doubt the integrity of a methodology that derives general observations from samples. Many believe that "shrewd resourceful lawyers can put together a Brandeis brief in support of almost any conceivable exercise of legislative judgment" (Geis 1962, p. 573). And some maintain that the social sciences will become useful to the legal profession only when they "achieve the rigor of the most advanced of the physical sciences" (Donnelly 1959, p. 83). But the focus of the social sciences and the very nature of the subject matter renders such an achievement virtually impossible.

In addition, many lawyers are wary of the dissension among social scientists, believing that it reflects deep-seated defects in the social science disciplines themselves. From the time of the first uses of social science evidence, this belief has prevailed:

[W]hile courts will go a long way in admitting expert testimony deduced from a well-recognized scientific principle or discovery, the thing from which the deduction is made must be sufficiently established to have gained general acceptance in the particular field in which it belongs (*Frye v. United States*, 293 F. 1013, 1014 [D.C.Cir. 1923]).

As a result, they fear that the use of evidence as controversial and as impermanent as much of the social science research has proven to be would leave the determination of the law in an extremely uncertain state. They ask, "Can we afford, can we undertake every generation . . . to rewrite our statutes and our legislation when the sociological or psychiatric or medical theory changes?" (Kramer 1959, p. 568).

It has been alleged that part of the hostility toward social science evidence stems from territorial protectiveness—a defense against the increasing encroachment of the social sciences upon legal preserves. But the case against social science is not limited to subjective reactions. To a large degree, the antagonism of lawyers toward the social sciences springs from the inability of these sciences to provide pragmatic information directly relevant to the practice of law. Indeed, social research is most effective in those areas of law that affect a substantial portion of society, such as school segregation. In contrast, social research is much less valuable in cases that directly affect a limited number of individuals, such as cases determining criminality. Since the former category constitutes only a segment of the legal spectrum, social research can claim only a limited jurisdiction.

JUDICIAL REACTION

Not only have attorneys used social science evidence to convince judges and juries, but, on occasion, judges have incorporated results of social science research into their opinions to convince the public as well. It is a logical assumption that the actual role of social science research has been not in directing court actions but in supporting them. In fact, in controversial cases when opinions relating to social issues have broken with precedent, social science evidence has often been cited, quite plausibly, to buttress the opinion of the court, lend legitimacy to a result decided on other grounds, and counteract the emotional reaction of the public (see *Brown v. Board of Education*). As stated by Judge Bazelon (1977) of the District of Columbia Court of Appeals: "when the issues are controversial, any decision may fail to satisfy large portions of the community. But those who are dissatisfied with a particular decision will be more likely to acquiesce in it if they perceive that their views and interests were given a fair hearing. If the decision maker has frankly laid the competing considerations on the table . . . he is unlikely to find himself accused of high handedness, deceit or cover-up."

However, even when the social research is well presented, judicial apprehension remains an uncertain factor. On the Supreme Court, five judges who are impressed with the social science research are frequently balanced by four who are not. In the lower courts, the variations are more extreme. And this uncertainty holds no promise of becoming clearer in the future. "We shall not know to what extent judges are significantly influenced by social science testimony until they tell us, and this is not customary, expedient, nor even wise from the standpoint of their relation to the public and to the losing party" (Rose 1955, p. 214).

CONCLUSION

Whatever the purpose in using the research, the impact of social science on the law is an identifiable factor that will grow as the cooperation of social science and the law further develops (Cohen 1948, p. 501):

While we come to the present century we see emerging as the dominant philosophical system the doctrine of *pragmatism* [which] . . . insists that beyond and beneath legal forms are human interests pressing for recognition. Law comes to be regarded as an agency of social control, one among many. . . . Legal philosophy becomes a theory of social interests and social psychology takes up where law leaves off.

REFERENCES

Allport, F. (1953) The effects of segregation and the consequences of desegregation: a social science statement. Appendix to appellant's brief in *Davis v. County School Board*. 1952. 37 *Minn. L. Rev.* 427.

Armour, D. (1972) The evidence on busing. *The Public Interest* Summer:90–126.

Bazelon, D. L. (1977) Coping with technology through the legal process. *Cornell Law Review* 62(5):817–32.

Bohrer, R. A. (1973) Educational testing: a challenge for the courts. *University of Illinois Law Forum* 2:375–88.

Botein, D. (1965) The Manhattan Bail Project: its impact on criminality and the criminal law process. *Texas Law Review* 43:319.

Cahn, E. (1955) Jurisprudence. *New York University Law Review* 30:150.

Clinard, M. (1951) Sociologists and American criminology. *Journal of Criminal Law* 41:549–77.

Cohen, J. (1943) Labor-welfare cases: a socio-legal approach. *University of Chicago Law Review* 10(4):375–416.

Coleman, J. S., et al. (1966) *Equality of Education Opportunity*. U.S. Department of Health, Education, and Welfare. Washington, D.C.: U.S. Government Printing Office.

Cowan, T. A. (1948) Relation of law to experimental social science. *University of Pennsylvania Law Review* 92:484–502.

Cullison, A. D. (1969) Identification by probabilities and trial by arithmetic. *Houston Law Review* 6:471.

Donnelly, R. C. (1959) Some comments upon the law and behavioral science program at Yale. *Journal of Legal Education* 12:83.

Edison, M. (1970) The empirical assault on capital punishment. *Journal of Legal Education* 23:2.

Finkelstein, M. O., and Fairley, W. B. (1970) A Bayesian approach to identification evidence. *Harvard Law Review* 83(3):489.

Garfinkel, H. (1959) Social science evidence and the school segregation cases. *Journal of Politics* 21(1):37–59.

Geis, G. (1962) Social science and the law. *Washburn Law Journal* 1:569–86.

Gibbons, H. (1971) Law in an age of social change. *American Bar Association Journal* 57:151.

Greenberg, J. (1956) Social scientists take the stand. *Michigan Law Review* 54:953.

Handler, J. F. (1971) Field research strategies in urban legal studies. *Law and Society Review* 5:345.

Hindelang, M. (1972) On the methodological rigor of the Bellamy Memorandum. *Criminal Law Bulletin* 8(6):507.

Hobson, J. A. (1910) *The Evolution of Modern Capitalism*. New York: Charles Scribner.

Kingston, C. R. (1966) Probability and legal proceedings. *Journal of Criminal Law*. 57:93.

Kramer, R. (1959) Some observations on law and interdisciplinary research. *Duke Law Journal* Fall:563.

Lochner, P. R., Jr. (1973) Some limits on the application of social science research in the legal process. *Law and Social Order* (1973):815–48.

Ravitch, D. (1975) Busing: the solution that has failed to solve. *New York Times News of the Week in Review* December 21, p. 3.

Reiss, A. J., Jr. (1970) Law and sociology: some issues for the 70s. *University of Richmond Law Review* 5:31.

Robbins, I. (1975) the admissability of social science evidence in person-oriented adjudication. *Indiana Law Journal* 50:493.

Rose, A. M. (1955) The social scientist as an expert witness. *Minnesota Law Review* 40:205.

Tribe, L. H. (1971) A further critique of mathematical proof. *Harvard Law Review* 84:1810.

Zeisel, H. (1959) The uniqueness of survey evidence. *Cornell Law Quarterly* 45:322.

Zeisel, H., and Diamond, S.S. (1974) Convincing empirical evidence on the six member jury. *University of Chicago Law Review* 41:281–95.

Ziskind, D. (1939) The use of economic data in law cases. *University of Chicago Law Review* 6:607.

X